THE TOURIST IN YOSEMITE

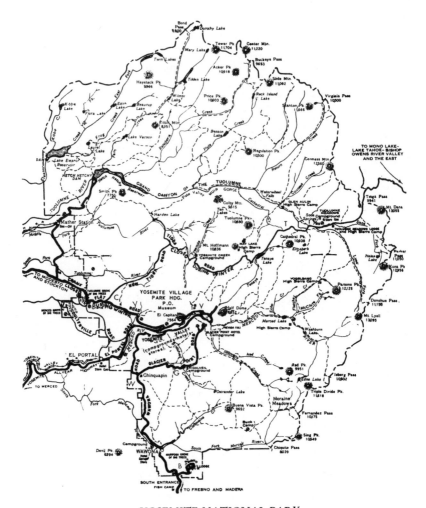

YOSEMITE NATIONAL PARK

Figure 1. From *Self-guiding Auto Tour of Yosemite National Park*, a special issue of *Yosemite Nature Notes*, June 1956.

The Tourist in Yosemite, 1855-1985

Stanford E. Demars

University of Utah Press
Salt Lake City, Utah
1991

∞ The paper in this book meets the standards for permanence and durability established by the Committee on Production Guidelines for Book Longevity of the Council on Library Resources

Library of Congress Cataloging-in-Publication Data

Demars, Stanford E., 1942-
    The tourist in Yosemite, 1855-1985 / Stanford E. Demars.
        p.   cm.
    Includes bibliographical references and index.
    ISBN 0-87480-367-5 (cloth : alk. paper)
    1. Yosemite National Park (Calif.)—History. 2. Travelers—
California—
Yosemite National Park—History. 3. Tourist trade—California—
Yosemite National Park—History. 4. Wilderness areas—United States—
Public opinion—History. 5. Public opinion—United States—History. I.
Title.
F868.Y6D44 1991
917.94'4704—dc20   90-47262
                                                                    CIP

Illustrations in this book are from the collection in the research library at Yosemite National Park, and are used with permission.

Contents

Preface

To BORROW AN OLD YANKEE adage, this book has been a long time a'borning. It began as a doctoral dissertation during those turbulent, often disturbing days of the latter 1960s when Yosemite Valley was an open conflict zone between the establishment and the flower children of the counter-culture movement. When this conflict erupted into violence over the Independence Day weekend of 1970, it signalled to many old-time Yosemite lovers that the park they had come to love so well had both figuratively and literally gone to pot. The unpleasantness of those experiences, along with an employment move to New England, left me with little desire to continue my Yosemite studies. Consequently, I abandoned them in favor of pursuing further the roots of North American attitudes toward nature and pleasurable use of the scenic outdoors. As it turned out, a chance encounter with Peirce Lewis, then president of the Association of American Geographers, rendered this abandonment a temporary one. Dr. Lewis had kindly taken the opportunity to read the dissertation some years earlier, and when we met again at a regional geographers conference in the fall of 1983, chastized me rather severely for not seeing my Yosemite work through to book-length publication. In a very real sense, then, the appearance of this book is due to him and his thoughtful concern for the work of a younger colleague.

I would like to acknowledge with gratitude the Rhode Island College Faculty Research Committee for providing me with several much-needed travel grants. Special thanks are due also to Dr. David Greene, dean of the college's Faculty of Arts and Sciences, for his willingness to defray the costs of the photographs. As he himself observed, he is probably the only person in New England to have read both the dissertation and the manuscript of the book. Dr. Jan van Wagtendonk, director of the Yosemite Research Institute, was more than kind in offering me not only the facilities of the Institute but also the unrestricted use of that most indispensable of all research tools, the charge card to the National Park Service copy machine. I am also indebted to the many other Park Service personnel at Yosemite who took time out of busy summer schedules to both answer my questions and provide additional insights. Most of all, I am grateful for the patience, unfailing courtesy, and enormous assistance given me by what must be the Park Service's premier research librarian, Mary Vocelka. As a member of an enormously competent but inevitably under-appreciated profession, she is without peer. It is difficult to imagine this book without her help. Lastly, I would be remiss in not publicy thanking my wife and family for their role in seeing this project through to completion. It is to my children and theirs after them that this book is dedicated, in the hope that they, also, will have the opportunity to know and love the "Incomparable Valley" and all that is associated therewith.

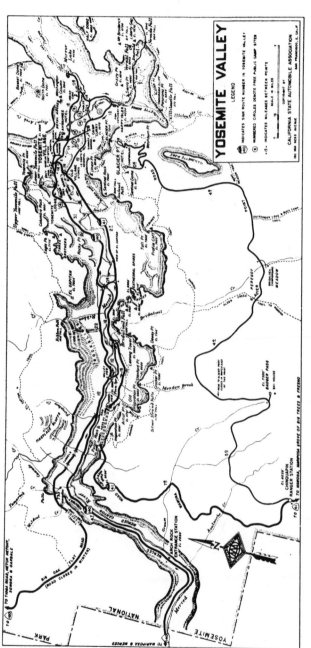

HIGHWAY DISTANCES FROM YOSEMITE MUSEUM, YOSEMITE VALLEY

Yosemite Valley Area (see above map)

Ahwahnee Hotel	.8 mi.	Housekeeping Camp	1.0 mi.
Bridalveil Fall	4.5 mi.	El Capitan Bridge	3.5 mi.
Camp Curry	1.4 mi.	Happy Isles	2.5 mi.
Camp 4 (public campground)	.8 mi.	Mirror Lake	.7 mi.
Camp 7 (public campground)	1.0 mi.	Old Village (store, etc.)	.7 mi.
Camp 9 (organization camp)	1.5 mi.	Pohono Bridge	5.6 mi.
Camp 11 (public campground)	1.8 mi.	Curry Company stables	1.9 mi.
Camp 12 (public campground)	1.9 mi.	Wawona Tunnel (east portal)	6.0 mi.
Camp 14 (public campground)	1.8 mi.	Yosemite Falls parking area	.7 mi.
Camp 15 (public campground)	1.0 mi.	Yosemite Lodge	.6 mi.

Points Outside Yosemite Valley Area

Arch Rock Ranger Station	11.0 mi.	Mono Lake	76.0 mi.
Badger Pass (winter ski area)	20.0 mi.	Reno (via Tioga Road)	218.0 mi.
Fresno (via Wawona Road)	94.0 mi.	(via All-Year Highway and Sacramento)	334.0 mi.
Glacier Point	30.0 mi.	San Francisco (via All-Year Highway)	211.0 mi.
Hetch Hetchy (via B.O. Flat Rd.)	38.0 mi.	(via Big Oak Flat Road)	195.0 mi.
Los Angeles (via Wawona Road)	313.0 mi.	South Entrance Ranger Station	31.0 mi.
(via All-Year Highway)	356.0 mi.	Tioga Pass Ranger Station	62.0 mi.
(via Tioga Pass)	418.0 mi.	Tuolumne Meadows	55.0 mi.
Mariposa (All-Year Highway)	44.0 mi.	Wawona	27.0 mi.
Merced (via All-Year Highway)	81.0 mi.		
Mariposa Grove (Wawona Road)	36.0 mi.		

Figure 2. From *Self-guiding Auto Tour of Yosemite National Park*, June 1956.

Chapter 1
Introduction

MY WIFE AND I FIRST ARRIVED at the Arch Rock entrance to Yosemite National Park in June of 1968. It was an auspicious time to be in Yosemite. Nearly one hundred years earlier John Muir had arrived in the Valley to begin his life-long obsession with the Yosemite and what he thought it ought to represent in American culture. Just one century later, if what one read in the newspapers was true, the place that Muir had loved above all others was experiencing something of a crisis. To begin with there simply seemed to be too many people for the restricted confines of Yosemite Valley. Particularly congested were the Village shopping areas and the campgrounds, where long lines of hopeful but likely to be disappointed newcomers waited like vultures to pounce upon newly-vacated campsites. Parking space was at a premium, at best, and non-existent, at worst. Frustrated motorists in many cases simply pulled their vehicles off the roads and left them parked wherever they could find a spot big enough, regardless of all signs and restrictions that prohibited such practice.

As disturbing as the numbers of people were the activities in which they were engaged. In many ways the Yosemite Valley of the late 1960s reflected more the noise and honky-tonk of an urban amusement park than the pristine beauty and wildness of a national park. Drag racing teenagers, pot parties, and rock band concerts vied for attention with Half Dome, the Merced River, and the interpretive efforts of the National Park Service. Equally disturbing, at least to me, was the barbed-wire enclosed bastion of elitism that was the Ahwahnee Hotel. Standing on the underprivileged side of the fence, watching fashionably dressed dowagers playing a leisurely round of golf, I felt angry and frustrated by what seemed to be a colossal case of mismanagement. How could the Park Service possibly condone, in a tiny place like Yosemite Valley, the use of a barbed-wire enclosure that looked like it was designed to separate the privileged from the public? (The fence had not been built for that purpose—originally it had been intended to protect the Ahwahnee flower gardens from the depredations of the Valley's deer population.) Furthermore, what right did any group of visitors, whether the Ahwahnee crowd or the noisily vulgar marijuana smokers, have to treat a national park in the way that Yosemite was being treated? How could the National Park Service, entrusted with the care and management of what were arguably the nation's most precious natural resources, permit such a travesty upon the national park idea?

In defense of the National Park Service it must be pointed out that the situation was far from being as simple as it appeared to a rather naive graduate student. As part of the enabling legislation of 1916 the National Park Service was given the charge to manage the parks with a dual purpose:

> The service thus established should promote and regulate the use of the Federal areas known as national parks, monuments, and reservations hereinafter specified by such means and measures as conform to the fundamental purposes of the said parks, monuments, and reservations, which purpose is to *conserve* the scenery and the natural and historic objects and the wildlife therein and to *provide for the enjoyment* of the same in such manner and by such means as will leave them unimpaired for the enjoyment of future generations. (*Emphasis added.*)[1]

To the founders of the National Parks Act conserving the parks largely meant protecting them from such traditionally exploitative interests as lumber and mining companies. Given the low level of use of most of the parks it was probably not anticipated that future visitor pressures might one day pose a threat to their preservation. It is even more unlikely that the Service's founders could have imagined the extent to which the meaning of the word "enjoyment" would change in the coming decades. By the latter 1960s, "enjoyment" of the Yosemite had come to include everything from backpacking in the High Sierra wilderness to taking a guided bus tour around the Valley floor; from scaling a granite cliff to playing a leisurely round of golf; from joining a guided nature hike to attending an evening night club show; from sleeping on the ground and eating canned beans to luxuriating in what was advertised as one of the resort world's most elegant hotels; from spending a quiet hour in a library to jostling for space along the crowded banks of the Merced River; from dancing to the decimating decibels of a rock band to lounging in a shaded lawn chair; from watching portable television in a camp trailer to enjoying a scenic movie at a nearby hotel; from fishing in a secluded alpine lake to playing a fast game of tennis;

Figure 3. Golfers through the fence at the Ahwahnee Hotel grounds.

and from feasting on the scenic splendor of Yosemite Falls and Half Dome to getting stoned on a variety of psychedelic drugs. The list could go on and on. The problem that the National Park Service faced was largely one of definition. Who was to say what constituted "enjoyment" of Yosemite or any other national park? The only legal limitations imposed upon visitor enjoyment of parks were contained in the charge to manage them so as to leave them "unimpaired for the enjoyment of future generations." Over the years that has left, needless to say, room for a tremendous variety of interpretations. It is these interpretations, along with their origins and principal characteristics, that are the topic of this book. Expressed somewhat differently, this book is about the visitor experience in Yosemite National Park and how it has changed over the 130 years or so that Yosemite has functioned as a scenic attraction.

It is perhaps axiomatic that one's perception of something has a direct bearing on the extent to which one finds enjoyment in that something. Simply put, if a person perceives ice cream to be a truly delectable dessert it is likely that he will find enjoyment in eating it. Similarly, for the small boy who dislikes liver there are few things that can equal the revulsion he feels when confronted by a plate heaping with liver and onions. In many cases our perception of something is determined by factors unrelated to the actual qualities or attributes of the something in question. For example, there is nothing inherently good-tasting about ice cream, just as there is nothing inherently objectionable about liver or, for that matter, raw grubs, fresh blood or any one of a number of foods that are regularly consumed by members of the human species. As any beginning anthropology student knows, human prejudices for or against food are mainly learned from others. This is not to say that our taste buds do not act as a defensive mechanism by discouraging our consumption of, say, a meat product that has become putrid. Rather it is to suggest that human taste buds are not the most important discriminator in the determination of diet. After all, more than one hapless hominid has discovered to his regret that food tainted with botulism-producing bacteria did not taste like it.

There are many characteristics of human societies that, like diet preferences, are passed from one generation or individual to another as *learned behavior*. The ability of human beings to communicate such behavior is dependent upon our ability to attach meaning to specific symbols and to utilize those symbols as language. While language, be it oral or written, is the principal medium of human communication, it is by no means the only one. Within any given society there are gestures, scents, and pictorial representations that facilitate effective communication between individuals and/or groups. The term that is used to describe the human characteristics that represent learned values and behaviors is *culture*. Culture is variously described as including a people's belief systems (religious, political), institutions (legal, governmental, social), and technology (skills, use of tools and/or equipment). Culture represents the sum of acquired knowledge that is used to interpret and give meaning to life and the world in which we live. In addition, (and this is of fundamental importance to this book), *culture is the most important determinant influencing what we as human beings perceive as esthetically pleasing or displeasing*. Most of us have seen a National Geographic magazine article that illustrates the extent to which certain physical attributes, such as elongated necks, flattened heads, or extreme obesity, are perceived as particularly attractive within the context of a culture group. To many of us the idea that these features add to a person's attractiveness is preposterous. Yet few of us

4

are able to recognize the elements within our own society that are valued in purely subjective terms and which may be equally preposterous to people outside our culture—such as men's neckties and ladies' high-heeled shoes.

Students of geography have long been aware of the extent to which cultural perceptions of nature have influenced the conduct of human populations. The ways that people have reacted toward, utilized, and sought to modify the environments in which they have lived have been largely a function of cultural prejudices and value systems. For example, the perception of wild nature, or wilderness, as something to be feared and conquered was a notion that dominated the Western world for centuries. Only rather recently has wilderness come to be perceived as pleasing. Also of rather recent vintage is the notion that mountains have esthetic value. Our medieval ancestors abhorred them as excrescential abominations whose existence served principally as reminders of what mankind had lost as a result of the Fall. The fact remains that what we as human beings perceive as esthetically pleasing in nature is of cultural derivation; as such our notions of what is scenically attractive are no more absolute or impervious to change than any other cultural phenomena.

This is particularly true in the case of the national park idea. The entire concept of a national park, of landscape set aside to preserve an assemblage of features for largely esthetic reasons, is a notion that is eminently cultural. That we should recognize it as such in no way belittles or demeans what is perhaps as admirable a cultural achievement as any in our history. What is important to remember is that there is no absolute system of values that is associated with the national park idea. Neither is any particular means of enjoying a national park intrinsically better or worse than any other—only by definition of what we want our parks to be can we determine what is an "appropriate" way to use and enjoy our national park heritage. As we shall see in the following chapters of this book that definition has changed significantly over the years. Furthermore, there is reason enough to expect that it will continue to change in the future.

Since its discovery by tourists in the 1850s Yosemite illustrates better than any other park the ways in which we as Americans have perceived and utilized our national park heritage. That these perceptions and utilizations are and will continue to be culturally based is the thesis of this book. It is my hope that by developing a sense of historical and cultural context readers will come to a better understanding of what the Yosemite means to us. In the process we cannot help but become more conscientious stewards of what is rightfully acknowledged as one of the world's unique places.

In the first chapter of this book I have tried to set forth the primary ingredients of the Yosemite "problem." The importance of culture and cultural perception have been stressed in the hope that the reader will be able to extricate himself from the usual blinders of cultural subjectivity and view the national park idea and its manifestations in Yosemite in as dispassionately objective a way as possible. Chapter Two is an attempt to place the discovery of Yosemite for tourist purposes in its proper historical and cultural context. Of particular importance in this regard were the philosophical and practical expressions of romanticism, the dominant mode of nature interpretation of the nineteenth century pleasure traveler. It is the contention of Chapter Three that the Yosemite of the latter nineteenth century functioned essentially as a contemporary romantic pleasure resort and that many of the characteristics of romantic Yosemite would persist into the twentieth century. The role of the Yosemite Valley commissioners as perpetrators of traditional modes of nature appreciation is discussed along with the tensions that arose between them and subsequent generations of nature lovers. Chapter Four deals with the growth of the outdoors movement. While essentially romantic in origin the notion of enjoying the Great Outdoors in a physically rigorous way signalled a major departure from traditional approaches to enjoying natural scenery. John Muir and the Sierra Club, along with David Curry and the tent camps, are discussed as we trace the influence upon visitor perception and habits of the growing propensity of Americans to spend their leisure time outdoors. Chapter Five begins with the establishment of the National Parks Act in 1916. In Yosemite, as in other national parks, the newly-created National Park Service served not only to institutionalize existing perceptions and use patterns but also to develop and popularize the parks to an extent scarcely imaginable to previous generations of park people. The formal establishment of the nature interpretation program reflected the developing sense that the national parks represented the best of American culture and landscape heritage, something that would prove to be perhaps its most persistent theme. In chapter Six we trace the post-World War II rise of the wilderness movement and its influence upon contemporary perception and utilization of Yosemite. In the final chapter I exercise an author's prerogative to both evaluate the past and make recommendations for future action. In every case I try to take the largest possible view with regard to both Yosemite and the national parks in general.

This is a book about Yosemite; discussion of other parks, as well as matters of national concern, is included primarily to provide context in order that the reader might more fully understand the development of the Yosemite story. Furthermore, this book differs from the approach of national park scholars who maintain that it has taken more than a century for the "true"—i.e., "wilderness"—value of the parks to be rightfully appreciated. Such a stance is not only a bit myopic but intellectually untenable since it presupposes something that is unsupported by natural science—that there are absolute definitions of "right" and "wrong" in nature. Natural phenomena, whether animate or inanimate, are far too complex to be managed—if, in fact, they so should be—under such restrictive parameters. All well-intended sentiment notwithstanding, the national park idea is a cultural notion that has value only in a cultural context. To claim otherwise is as unwise as it is unfair to those who have influenced its creation and development. This book is an effort to present the story of Yosemite within the context of its own time and place. Sincere effort has been made to represent each generation of Yosemite tourists, their perceptions, their habits, their foibles and their strengths, from as objective a viewpoint as possible. I have done this for several reasons. Not only is it better scholarship to do so, but it also seems to be the only humane way to discuss people who, for the most part, wanted little more than to enjoy for themselves the uniqueness and beauty of the Yosemite.

Figure 4. "Descent Into the Valley," from *Appleton Magazine*, 1873.

Chapter 2

The Discovery of the "Yo Semite"

DURING THE WINTER OF 1860–61 there appeared in a prominent Boston newspaper a series of articles written by a recent emigrant from that city to the Pacific coast. The name of the author was well known to New Englanders. Minister, orator, public servant, Thomas Starr King was also widely known for his gifted interpretations of natural scenery. His most recent book, a guide to the White Mountains of New Hampshire, was generally acknowledged to be the definitive work on that part of New England. Starr King's articles in the *Boston Evening Transcript* were in the form of letters describing a recent foray into California's Sierra Nevada Mountains. With what must have been considerable interest his readers followed his description of mountain scenery which, if it could be believed, surpassed anything the East or even Europe had to offer. The "Yo-Semite," a cleft or gorge in the wild Sierra Nevada, was the object of his descriptions, and he had been virtually overcome by the scenic wonders he had encountered. "How can I express the awe and joy that were blended and continually struggling with each other," he wrote, "during the half hour in the hot noon that we remained on the edge of the abyss where the grandeurs of the Yo-Semite were first revealed to us?" In summing up the impact that the Yosemite had made upon him, King felt impelled to quote from a recent report to the California State Agricultural Society, to which he added: "Shall I attempt to improve on that? No, verily."

> We will not attempt any description of "the thing." "The thing" is "there" away up in the Sierras, and all we have to say is that he who has threaded the streets of Nineveh and Herculaneum, scaled the Alps, and counted the stars from the top of Egypt's pyramids, measured the Parthenon, and watched the setting sun from the dome of St. Peter's, looked into the mouth of Vesuvius, and taken the key-note of his morning song from the thunder of Niagara, and has not seen the Yo-Semite, is like the Queen of Sheba before her visit to King Solomon—the half has not been told him.[1]

Starr King's enthusiastic account of the Yosemite country was not the first to reach the East Coast. The October 8, 1856 issue of the

Country Gentleman had republished an article from the *California Christian Advocate* which declared the "Yo-hem-i-ty" Valley to be "the most striking natural wonder on the Pacific" and predicted that it would eventually become a place of great resort.[2] In 1855 and 1856 a California pioneer artist, Thomas A. Ayres, had made his first sketches of Yosemite Valley; some of these were lithographed and spread widely over the East. An illustrated guide to American travel published in 1856 referred to Yosemite's scenery as "perhaps the most remarkable in the United States, and perhaps in the world."[3]

Along with Starr King's articles in the *Transcript*, the foregoing suggest that within a decade of its "discovery" by white Californians in 1851, the region known as "the Yosemite" was receiving widespread attention. Indeed, by the outbreak of the Civil War Yosemite had achieved the status of a "must" to be included in the itinerary of any fashionable visit to the Far West. During an 1860 trip to the Pacific coast, no less a personality than Horace Greeley succumbed to the temptation to include a visit to Yosemite in his already over-crowded agenda. Against the advice of local residents, who felt that the rewards of such a trip were not commensurate with the costs, Greeley rode approximately sixty miles by mule-back in one day, entering Yosemite Valley long after dark. Reaching the hotel sometime after one A.M., he was lifted painfully from his saddle and put straightway to bed without food or other refreshment. Arising "early" the next morning, he made a quick tour of the Valley and was on his way back to Stockton by noon. Despite this remarkably brief encounter, Greeley felt enamored enough with his new discovery to exclaim, "I know no single wonder of nature on earth which can claim superiority over the Yosemite."[4]

Another enthusiastic proponent of Yosemite was the transplanted Englishman James M. Hutchings. As editor of the *California Magazine*, Hutchings touted the wonders of Yosemite at every opportunity. Referred to by some as the "Father of Yosemite," he spent most of the last half-century of his life, from his first encounter with Yosemite in 1855 until his accidental death there in 1902, in more or less intimate association with Yosemite affairs. The various editions of his *Scenes of Wonder and Curiosity in California* not only acquainted readers with the scenic attractions of the Yosemite country but also did much to popularize and traditionalize the manner of visiting the area.

The enthusiastic publicity given Yosemite by such early promoters as Starr King, Greeley, and Hutchings contributed substantially to its acceptance as a popular tourist destination. Similar promotion resulted from a transcontinental trip made in 1865 by Samuel Bowles, editor of the *Springfield Republican*. In his book *Across the Continent*, Bowles elaborated to some extent upon the beauties of Yosemite, "the one unrivalled sublimity of nature in all the known world." In an introductory letter addressed to his traveling companion, Schuyler Colfax, then speaker of the House of Representatives, in which he reviewed practically all the scenic wonders they had seen in the West, Bowles asked if that "vision of Apocalypse so grand, so full of awe, so full of elevation, Yosemite Valley, does not stand out before all other sights, all other memories of this summer, crowded as it is with various novelty and beauty?" He went on to claim that "the world may well be challenged to match, in single sweep of eye, such impressive natural scenery as this. Indeed, it is not too much to say that no so limited space in all the known world offers such majestic and impressive beauty."[5]

At first glance such exuberance and use of superlatives seem excessive. Was the Yosemite really all that it was proclaimed to be? In order to understand both the grandiose style of early Yosemite description and the reception it achieved it is necessary to understand the audience for which such promotion was intended. Perception and utilization of scenic landscapes are subjective phenomena; as such they are directly related to and, indeed, are a function of the processes and characteristics of the culture group involved. In the case of Yosemite, before we can understand its establishment as a fashionable tourist destination we must come to grips with the values and habits of contemporary American leisure travel culture.

By the middle years of the nineteenth century there had emerged in the United States a well-established leisure society. Travel for pleasure constituted a significant component of this society and included annual visits to fashionable watering places, seaside resorts, and, increasingly, to such inland attractions as the Catskills and Niagara Falls. The pattern of activities associated with this travel followed precedents that had proven fashionable among the leisure elite of Europe. Indeed, for the first century and more of the new republic's existence its society leaders had seemed obsessed with the intent to mimic the "good life" as defined by fashion leaders on the other side of the Atlantic. The tendency to emulate European leisure lifestyles was particularly manifest in the ways in which Americans viewed nature and natural scenery. Specifically, nineteenth century American travel for pleasure was a function not only of traditional European perceptions of landscape beauty but also of the manner in which the dominant culture group chose to enjoy such beauty. English romanticism provided the philosophical basis for esthetic definitions, while a highly developed social consciousness and propensity to adhere to the dictates of travel fashion determined both the types of activities and the settings in which they took place.

During the first half of the nineteenth century American literature, especially as it related to nature and scenic beauty, was heavily influenced by such British romanticists as Samuel Coleridge, Sir Walter Scott, and William Wordsworth. American artists were similarly influenced, and the emergence of Thomas Cole and the Hudson River School of landscape painting were but American expressions—however potent—of a well-developed and intensely romantic philosophy of nature that was essentially European in origin. The romantic view of nature provided both an esthetic definition of scenery and a philosophical basis for the relationship of human beings to their natural world. Fundamental to the latter was the assumption that Man, as the foremost creation of Deity, occupied a pivotal position in what constituted attractiveness in the landscape. In both art and literature man and his creations constituted a considerable portion of what was considered scenic beauty.

Nature romanticism gave specific meaning to such scenic descriptors as beautiful, picturesque, and sublime—the most common terms used to depict romantic landscapes. "Beautiful" was often used by American travelers and writers to describe pastoral landscapes— low, rolling hills, smooth plains, carefully cultivated fields and gardens— graced, as it were, by the civilizing touch of man. "Picturesque," on the other hand, was used more for landscapes that were pleasingly varied, rough, rocky, and irregular in outline.[6] A landscape painting that was considered picturesque usually involved, in addition, a combination of depth and height that was framed by the artist to maintain a balance between the focus of the scene and its surrounding vertical and horizontal elements. To be truly picturesque required some evidence of the presence of man, the assumption being, of course, that such presence clearly depicted his harmony with as well as his mastery over the natural world. "Sublime," at first, implied much that was picturesque but on a grander scale. However, under the influence of Cole and others, "sublime" was used increasingly to refer to the "wild" in nature, and rather than focus on some work of man that gave meaning to the scene, romanticists tended to perceive a sublime landscape as a more direct expression of God Himself. Again, the matter of scale was important, as well as the greater element of mystery, of supernatural manifestation that engendered a more reverential perception of the natural scene. Well-recognized features of a wild, romantic landscape included references to amplitude or greatness of extent, vast and boundless prospects, great power and force exerted, the thundering cataract of violent storm, a great profusion of natural objects thrown together in wild confusion, obscurity, vagueness, indistinctness, darkness, mystery, suggestion of terror, evidences of cataclysmic force or superhuman power.[7]

Another distinguishing attribute of nature romanticists was the emotionalism that added to the intensity of both their appreciation of and relationship to nature. When confronted with a natural scene of established appeal, an appropriately romantic response was to be swept away by tide of emotion, as was Charlotte Bronte, in 1839, on the occasion of her first visit to the seaside. "The idea of seeing the SEA—of being near it—watching its changes by sunrise, sunset—moonlight—and noonday—in calm—perhaps in storm—fills and satisfies my mind," she wrote, and she was not disappointed. Indeed, she was so overwhelmed by the sight of it, she burst into tears and even when she had made "the sternest efforts" to subdue her emotions, was "very quiet and subdued for the remainder of the day."[8] Appropriate and intense emotional response to landscape was fundamental to the romantic interpretation of nature, particularly in the presence of scenery considered truly sublime.

Related to the emotional response to nature was the infatuation with historical and romantic associations. Particularly European in emphasis was the belief that the truly beautiful and/or picturesque landscape was one that had been hallowed by some event, personality, or artifact significant to the culture involved. "No city or landscape," declared Naipaul, "is truly real unless it has been given quality of myth by writer, painter, or by its association with great events."[9]

The necessity for some historic or romantic association to give meaning to a site was a pervasive characteristic of the romantic interpretation of natural scenery. Moreover, since emotional response to landscapes, particularly those sanctified by historical and romantic associations, was fundamental to a nature romanticist's perceptions of nature, it is not surprising that he sought to register such feelings in some appropriately expressive medium. In fact, the fashionable traveler was expected to be something of an artist, if not in his skill on canvas, at least in his ability to express himself in a literary mode. "Travels, to be good for anything, must be literary," pronounced the editors of the new *Magazine of Travel* in 1857.[10]

It is due largely to this characteristic of the nature romanticist that there exists such a volume of nineteenth century travel accounts. Criticized today as being overly sentimental, extravagantly flowery, and just plain misleading, in their cultural and chronological context such literature not only was appropriate but commendable expression of the dominant cultural theme. This characteristic of romanticism also helps explain the importance of such individuals as Starr King, whose gifted literary ability enabled him to establish a high esthetic standard of interpretation of the scenes he described. That his thoughts, reactions, and sentiments should be both revered and copied by subsequent travelers was only consistent with the romanticist's infatuation with association. According to Huth there gradually emerged all over the country a group of writers who reported their direct observations of nature. In order to justify his impressions, an early writer on nature might quote a romantic poet, such as Scott. He would perhaps tell of a traveler who entered a forest at a late hour and heard there the sound of a bugle. "This is truly a romantic scene," the writer thinks, because the situation reminds him of a novel by Scott he has just read.[11] The propensity to record one's impressions of nature pervaded all kinds of travel. Nineteenth century explorers to the Far West, emigrants, and sportsmen alike added their accounts to those of the leisure traveler. No author, it seemed, ever tired of describing the sublimity and the grandeur of the scenery and the enchantment produced by it. "To prose

Figure 5. A particularly romantic view: The Delaware Water Gap.

14

it here, to verse it there, and picturesque it every where" became a literary mannerism used to brighten many a poem or essay.[12]

One of the most keenly felt deficiencies in the new republic was the lack of an established social aristocracy. While it was true that the absence of royalty in America could be defined as either asset or liability, America's upper classes resented the allegation by socially conscious Europeans that theirs was a land of primitive social institutions peopled by an unsophisticated bourgeoisie. By the middle of the nineteenth century an aristocratic society of sorts had begun to emerge along the Atlantic seaboard. As might be expected, this society depended for its class distinction upon both accumulated wealth and traditional, more European discriminators of birth and position. An uneasy amalgam of self-made millionaires and "aristocrats" of inherited fortunes, this was the group which supplied the leisure travelers and nature romanticists of the day. Its members utilized their financial ability to pursue fashionable travel as but another means of insuring social differentiation in a nation that made much of democracy.

It was partly the desire of the wealthy to encourage social exclusivity that gave character to contemporary leisure habits. Then, as now, travel for pleasure was defined in terms of vacation as much as for sightseeing. Not only was such travel destination-oriented, but inherent in its basic purpose was the desire to escape from the disagreeable elements of everyday life. Nineteenth century leisure travelers welcomed opportunities to flee the increasing congestion and tedium of the city. Similarly, they relished escape from the disagreeable social

Figure 6. A romanic rendering of Bridal Veil Falls, Yosemite.

conditions which were becoming less the exception than the rule in contemporary urban America. To the socially self-conscious leisure classes of mid-nineteenth century America, the appeal of escape included the desire to avoid contact with social inferiors and, instead, to frequent those areas and circulate among those circles which enhanced social status.

High status areas, however (as well as the people who visited them), were notoriously vulnerable to the whims of fashion. Aspiring members of society followed closely the travel accounts of their social superiors and, when possible, sought to duplicate their experiences, sometimes as much for enhancement of status as for purposes of pleasure. In this respect the publication of the travel guides that were appearing by the 1850s and 1860s served a useful purpose, assuring travelers that competent and fashionable critics of scenery had preceded them and had already enshrined in words or paint those points worthy of their visit. Guides like Sweetser's *Book of Summer Resorts, explaining Where to Find Them, How to Find Them, and their Special Advantages* (from 1868 through the 1890s) became indispensable accouterments to leisure travel. Such guidebooks at times were accused of inhibiting as much as inspiring and assisting leisure travel. According to Earl Pomeroy, in his book *In Search of the Golden West*, tourists too often sought out only what the guidebook recommended, and according to schedule felt only the prescribed emotions: of satisfaction in having seen what "everyone" saw; and of wonder and awe at God's work and the turmoil of creation.[13] The fact remains that middle-nineteenth century leisure travel conformed closely to fashions dictated and influenced by the socially prominent and imaginative leaders of the day. The words of men like Starr King took on the aura of scripture, to be read and re-read by travelers embarking upon pilgrimages to scenic shrines.

By the middle of the century a definite pattern had emerged with regard to travel for pleasure. Largely dependent upon the comforts and expedience of steamboat and railroad transportation, travelers mostly frequented locations of acceptable social status. Such visits were usually extended in time and were part of a travel itinerary which might include a springtime interlude at a mineral water health spa, such as White Sulphur Springs, Virginia; a summer season at a fashionable seaside resort, such as Long Branch, New Jersey, or Newport, Rhode Island; and a late summer or early autumn visit up the Hudson River to Saratoga Springs or the Catskill Mountain House. Fundamental to an understanding of this travel was the fact that these locations functioned essentially as pleasure resorts, and furthermore, that the resort hotel was the focal point for the social interaction that gave substance to the romanticist's enjoyment of nature. Prevailing definitions of picturesque scenery suggested that the hotel, with its expansive verandas, occupy a location of central prominence. Such a siting not only epitomized the romantic expression of man's relationship to nature but also functioned rather more prosaically to insure him the best and usually least painfully obtained view of the surrounding landscape.

Another important attribute of resort hotel life was the degree to which it could maintain a socially controlled, which meant exclusive, environment. Indeed, much of the charm of a resort like Newport "was in large part that not everyone could enjoy it who wished to."[14] The class consciousness of the so-called "Gilded Age" tourist required, insofar as possible, "escape" from those elements deemed either undesirable or socially inferior; there was little place for democracy in contemporary leisure travel culture. Neither was there any desire on the part of most pleasure travelers to "rough it." The ability to maintain one's self in a manner befitting social prominence was of fundamental importance to nineteenth century travelers. Resort hoteliers vied with each other in their attempts to provide the most luxurious accommodations, the choicest cuisine, and the most elegant appointments possible. Such attractions served not only to attest to the social status of travelers but also to substantiate the function of pleasure resorts to provide an "ideal" lifestyle for their patrons.

Much can be learned about the Gilded Age tourist by analyzing the kinds of activities which occupied his time at a resort. Some of these, such as "taking the water" and bathing—be it in mineral, salt, or fresh water—had been popular from the beginning of romantic resort life. Others, such as pleasure boating on placid waters, or retiring to a scenic spot with one's sketch pad, were considered to be particularly romantic. In general, nature romanticists tended to engage in activities which were more intellectual than physical, more detached than participatory. Reading and contemplating the works of the great romantic literati, meditating in the presence of the sublime, and expressing one's emotions in verse or conversation were the substance of romantic interpretation and enjoyment of nature.

Geographically, a wide variety of scenic locations attracted the Gilded Age tourist. "Scenery," according to the definitions of the times, also included such works of man as great bridges, factories, railroad tunnels, and civic structures, with a pronounced emphasis upon sites and edifices of historical and cultural importance. Although in America the latter consisted mainly of Revolutionary War and other memorials relating to the "Founding Fathers," and would not have been considered truly picturesque or romantic by European standards, it was the best the American landscape had to offer, and the pride with which American travelers viewed these memorials was scarcely diminished by their historical or cultural shortcomings. Nevertheless, it should be emphasized that contemporary leisure travelers visited such sites only in passing; the principal destinations and the bulk of time spent in leisure travel involved the relatively few areas of scenic attraction deemed noteworthy by travel fashion leaders.

Earlier in the nineteenth century the emphasis had been upon mineral water health spas and seaside resorts, which had successfully united the concern for health restoration with social pleasure. Of the former, Stafford Springs, Connecticut, had been followed (and eclipsed) by the Virginia Springs (White, Sulphur, etc.) and Saratoga Springs, up the Hudson River Valley from New York City. Newport, in the north, and Cape May and Long Branch, New Jersey, in the south, were foremost among the society resorts at the seaside. By mid-century the restoration of health by partaking of mineral waters had all but been abandoned in favor of the more strictly pleasurable attractions of resort life. Leisure travel expanded to include inland resorts in the Catskills, Berkshires, and the White Mountains of New Hampshire. According to contemporary tastes, emphasis was upon those sites that were considered particularly picturesque or sublime in the combination of their natural and human characteristics. West of the Appalachians, despite efforts of local promoters, tourist attractions were still in a developmental stage. The Gilded Age tourist of the middle-nineteenth century preferred, for the most part, to devote his leisure travel attentions to those areas whose reputation for scenic superiority and social prominence were already well established; the majority of these, as has been noted, were concentrated north and east of the nation's capital.

As noted, intrinsic to nineteenth century American culture was the propensity to seek social inspiration from European arbiters of fashion. The desire to mimic European patterns of high culture leisure lifestyles was in part a manifestation of Americans' lack of cultural identity.[15] The very newness of the republic precluded the existence of great traditions in art, music, and literature, particularly as those media were popularly utilized to enshrine events and personalities of cultural prominence. In the context of romanticism, with its emphasis upon cultural and historic associations, American scenery was bound to fall short of its European counterpart. Advocates of American scenery grudgingly conceded this deficiency. "Although American scenery is often so fine we feel the want of associations such as cling to scenes in the old world," wrote Thomas Cole. "Simple nature is not quite sufficient. We want human interest, incident and action to render the effect of landscape complete."[16]

In his book *The Civilized Wilderness*, Edward Foster described the response of patriotic Americans loyal to their own landscape by suggesting that Americans seldom willingly admitted their inferiority in any respect, and it should hardly be surprising that many felt called on to prove that at least some American landscapes provided a wealth of associations. Lydia Howard Huntley Sigourney, a phenomenally popular poetess known as the "Sweet Singer of Hartford," reminded her readers that "though of comparatively recent date, many of (our country's) associations are as lofty and spirit-stirring as those which strike more deeply into the dimness of antiquity." The Knickerbocker poet Robert Sands claimed that in America "the local associations are many, and of deep interest. Some of them, too, are beginning to assume the rust of antiquity."[17] Attempts to provide American scenery with appropriately romantic associations exploited several themes. Foremost among these was the Revolutionary War, the event which, in the minds of Americans, most clearly epitomized their national definition of democracy and freedom. Thomas Cole, while admitting America's deficiencies in romantic associations, was quick to point out that "American scenes are not destitute of historical and legendary associations; the great struggle for freedom has sanctified many a spot, and many a mountain, stream, and rock, has its legend, worthy of the poet's pen or the painter's pencil."[18]

In the minds of many, the American Indian provided an even greater sense of antiquity. Lydia Mary Child in 1845 suggested a direct comparison with a popular European scenic icon when she wrote that "whenever you find a ruined monastery, or the remains of an Indian encampment, you may be sure you have discovered the loveliest site in all the surrounding landscape."[19] Although a cynic might have accused her of pushing the point, the intent of her defense is clear.

Notwithstanding Americans' attempts to the contrary, fashionable Europeans were in general unimpressed with the beauty and picturesque qualities of the American landscape. "I have just been seeing a number of landscapes by an American painter of some repute; and the ugliness of them is wonderful," related John Ruskin, the recognized European arbiter of taste, to his friend, Charles Eliot Norton, in 1856. "I see that they are true studies and that the ugliness of the country must be unfathomable." In 1871 Ruskin elaborated on his prejudices by stating that although he had "kind invitations enough to visit America, (he) could not even for a couple of months live in a country so miserable as to possess no castles."[20] While few Americans were likely to have been sympathetic to or appreciative of Ruskin's snobbery, many would have agreed with the publisher of *Godey's Magazine*, Sarah J. Hale, who felt that although "circumstances had almost inevitably designed us a nation of travelers" it was nonetheless true that many travelers who could be sensitive to natural beauties did not yet take to touring the country for lack of intellectual and "poetical" associations with the scenery.[21]

The success with which Americans sought to establish scenic attractions that could be considered truly beautiful and/or picturesque varied with the locale. In general, American seaside resorts were most successful in challenging the pre-eminent position of fashionable European travel destinations, particularly with the increasing opulence of places like Newport, Rhode Island. Inland, despite the unquestioned grandeur of Niagara Falls, American scenic landscapes were hard pressed to compete with the quaintness and charm of the English lakes country or the magnificence of alpine Switzerland. For a time the Catskill Mountain House overlooking the Hudson Valley was alluded to as "the Switzerland of America," while the Hudson River itself was widely touted as "the American Rhine." Such claims, however, were as often the cause for derision among experienced world travelers as they were justifications for national pride.

It was the superlative dimensions and grandeur of Niagara Falls that ultimately presaged the response of American nationalists to the charge that American scenery was deficient in picturesque beauty. Despite the falls' increasing commercial development, which was attracting both national and international criticism, it was nonetheless true that Europe had nothing which could compare to the awesome thunder and sheer volume of Niagara. In the context of romanticism, Niagara was more sublime than picturesque, more acclaimed for its grandeur than for its beauty. And in the sense that the "sublime" was more an expression of divine creation than a reflection of human artifact—no matter how picturesque—the status of Niagara Falls lent credence to the American propensity to minimize the visible presence of man as a necessary ingredient to scenic landscape. Simply stated, it confirmed what Americans had suspected all along: that America was, in fact, a nation of divine favor, and that just as its political and social aspirations were of a loftier plane than those of the Old World, so was it only natural that its scenery should represent definitions of beauty of a higher order. Furthermore, this argument suggested that much of what had hitherto proven an embarrassment, i.e., the raw newness and lack of development of the landscape, was, in fact, intrinsic to its scenic appeal. "If romanticists believed that nature could do no wrong even when it was 'raw' and chaotic," maintained Van Zandt, "the reason was that they also believed that nature was the spontaneous manifestation of a divine spiritual order as superior to anything man could create as the 'sublime' is to the lower order of the 'beautiful.'"[22]

Landscape that was "raw" and "wild"—wilderness, in the contemporary use of the term—was considered sublime only according to the scale of its features. The enormity of Niagara was its chief virtue, and until the middle third of the nineteenth century it stood alone as America's scenic attraction of undisputed international acclaim. Whereas the actual extent of the American landscape, with its vast assemblage of forest, river, and plain, suggested a certain sublimity and beauty, its very vastness rendered it almost incomprehensible to the leisure traveler of the romantic era. What was needed, if American claims of scenic superiority were to be justified on the basis of sublimity, were scenic attractions, like Niagara Falls, that were not only accessible but which could also combine magnitude of scale with conventionally attractive features in a setting that could be encompassed and appreciated by the romanticist mind. In short, what was needed were pleasure resorts in surroundings that were in harmony with contemporary perceptions of scenic beauty, but which offered attractions on a more monumental scale. The presence or absence of human artifact was of secondary importance; what was more important was the extent to which such landscapes could be considered truly sublime.

The opening of the Far West, with its astonishing array of natural wonders, provided Americans, at last, with claims to scenic superiority that were difficult to dispute. Everything "western" seemed to exist on a monumental scale. Boundless prairies teemed with numberless herds of buffalo, while giant rivers cut enormous chasms through towering ranges of snow-covered mountains. A great salt sea, similar to that of the Holy Land, bordered deserts whose vastness was surpassed only by the grotesque peculiarity of their life forms. In the West even the human elements seemed larger than life. Fantastic fortunes to be made by exploiting an almost unbelievable abundance of natural resources were accented by tales of suffering and hardship that cast human beings into vortices of massacre, starvation, and cannibalism. Places like Pike's Peak, the Garden of the Gods, the Great Salt Lake, and Yosemite Valley, along with the gold fields, polygamous Utah, and "celestial" San Francisco, were heralded as attractions without rival in the known tourist world. And with the promise of a transcontinental railroad sometime in the near future the expectation grew that the scenic extravagance of the Far West would soon be available to all but the most timid pleasure traveler.

These, then, were the principal cultural considerations which bore on the ease and rapidity with which Yosemite was established as a major scenic attraction and tourist destination: romantic perceptions of nature, a high degree of social consciousness, the popularity of resort life, and the obsession of anxiety-ridden American nationalists that American scenery achieve international recognition.

In June of 1864 Senator John Conness of California was persuaded by certain California gentlemen "of fortune, of taste, and of refinement" to introduce a bill which would grant the Yosemite Valley and the nearby Mariposa Grove of Giant Sequoia to the state of California. President Abraham Lincoln signed the act into law on June 29, 1864, and the Yosemite Valley Commission was created soon thereafter to manage the grant according to the directives contained in the legislation:

> That there . . . is hereby granted to the State of California the "cleft" or "gorge" . . . known as the Yo-Semite Valley . . . with the stipulation, nevertheless, . . . that the premises shall be held for public use, resort and recreation; shall be inalienable for all time . . . [23]

The commission's first chairman was the prominent easterner Frederick Law Olmsted, recently employed to manage General John Charles Fremont's estate in nearby Mariposa county. In his own right, Olmsted was more important as an arbiter of scenic landscape than either King, Greeley, or Bowles. As the landscape architect and artist who created New York City's Central Park, he only added to the prestige of Yosemite when he described a visit there during which he had been overcome by the "union of the deepest sublimity . . . with the deepest beauty of nature" which made "Yo Semite the greatest glory of nature."[24] It is likely that the status of Olmsted (he resigned the

Figure 7. Yosemite Valley from Mariposa Trail, 1871.

commission to return East in 1865) lent considerable prestige to the attractiveness and political novelty of the Yosemite grant.

While the efforts of Yosemite's early and fashionable advocates undoubtedly did much to bring the attractions of the area to the attention of the contemporary traveling world, in the long run it was the travelers themselves and how they perceived Yosemite's attractions that consolidated Yosemite's reputation as superlative scenic landscape. To the nineteenth century leisure traveler, the cliffs, waterfalls, giant trees, and gently meandering streams of Yosemite Valley bespoke the very essence of romantic landscape. This interpretation was enhanced immeasurably by the works of such artists as Thomas Ayres, Albert Bierstadt, and Thomas Hill, whose striking paintings both enhanced and exaggerated those elements of landscape most in harmony with contemporary nature romanticism. In a literary mode, accounts by early travelers abounded with typically romantic impressions:

> The Yosemite! As well interpret God in thirty-nine articles as portray it to you by word of mouth or pen. As well reproduce castle or cathedral by a stolen frieze, or broken column, as this assemblage of natural wonder and beauty by photograph or painting. The overpowering sense of the sublime, of awful desolation, of transcending marvelousness and unexpectedness,

that swept over us, as we reined our horses sharply out of green forests, and stood upon high jutting rock that overlooked this rolling, upheaving sea of granite mountains, holding far down its rough lap this vale of beauty of meadow and grove and river,—such tide of feeling, such stoppage of ordinary emotions comes at rare intervals in any life. It was the confrontal of God face to face, as in great danger, in solemn, sudden death. It was Niagara, magnified. All that was mortal shrank back, all that was immortal swept to the front and bent down in awe.[25]

While most early visitors seemed to agree that in Yosemite they had experienced the quintessence of scenic sublimity, they were also quick to point out that the area was not lacking in manifestations of the picturesque. "My own impression," said a visitor asked for his sensations on first beholding the Yosemite, "so skillfully is the view arranged for pictorial effect, was that of looking upon some perfect picture."[26] Travel guide authors sought constantly to assure their prospective market of Yosemite's picturesque qualities. In *The Yosemite Guide*

Figure 8. "Valley Ford of the Yo Semite." From *In the Heart of the Sierra*, 1888.

Book State Geologist J. D. Whitney maintained that a "majority of cultivated lovers of natural scenery" would admit the Yosemite Fall to surpass any in the world as presenting the most "perfect combinations of all the elements of the picturesque." Certainly, he claimed, taking the whole region of the Yosemite together, "it must be allowed that, in this particular kind of scenery, it is a locality without a rival in the world."[27]

The comments of James M. Hutchings are illustrative on several counts. Not only are his descriptions vivid portrayals of what constituted contemporary definitions of "picturesque" but, as a native Englishman, he was assumed to speak with some authority as to what could be considered truly picturesque by European standards. In typically romantic terms he described a ford across the Merced River as one of the most "beautifully picturesque scenes that eye ever saw. The oak, dogwood, maple, cottonwood, and other trees, form an arcade of

Figure 9. "Cathedral Spires." From *Picturesque America*, 1872

25

great beauty over the sparkling, rippling, pebbly stream, and, in the background, the lower fall of the Yo-Semite is dropping its sheet of snowy sheen behind a dark middle distance of pines and firs."[28]

Some of the area's early proponents, especially Hutchings, went so far as to suggest that Yosemite's attractions included romantic associations. Although admittedly more implicit than explicit, these associations could be imagined as superior to European attractions as the deistic sublime was superior in its essential grandeur to the more humanized picturesque. Among the most commonly touted of Yosemite's romantic associations were the Cathedral Rocks and Cathedral Spires, which were said to unite the "great impressiveness, the beauty, and the fantastic form of the Gothic architecture." Their shape and color suggested to Samuel Bowles the impression of standing among the ruins of "an old Gothic cathedral, to which those of Cologne and Milan are but baby-houses."[29] James Hutchings saw in one group of peaks the "dilapidated front of some grand old cathedral, with towers and buttresses, and a circle that strong imagination can make into a clock which will indicate the time of day to a moment!"[30]

Recognizing that such associations were more creative than convincing, writers like Hutchings chose usually to emphasize associations of a more substantive and, incidentally, more uniquely American character. The mystique of the American Indian was a popular subject for this type of association, and was often incorporated toponymically into Yosemite's most attractive features. Such was the case of Sentinel Rock, "a lofty and solitary peak, upon which the watchfires of the Indians have often been lighted to give warnings of approaching danger."[31] Perhaps because of his European upbringing, Hutchings was more infatuated than most with the romantic imagery of the aboriginal Yosemite landscape. He particularly appreciated "the beautiful and expressive" Indian place names of Yosemite features, even to the point of preferring the Indian "Pohono" to the admittedly romantic "Bridal Veil" because of its association with a mysterious Indian legend.

Within a decade or so of its first visit by a "purely" tourist party Yosemite emerged as one of America's premier scenic landscapes. In all the elements of the sublime, in particular, but with respectable attributes of the picturesque, Yosemite's attractions were offered as the American apotheosis of fashionable romantic scenery.

Chapter 3
A Romantic Pleasure Resort

THE COMPLETION OF THE TRANSCONTINENTAL railroad in 1869 removed the last substantive barrier to reasonable, if not completely comfortable, travel to the Pacific Coast. Among the earliest to take advantage of these improvements were journalists and politicians anxious to acquaint themselves with the wonders of the Far West. Following closely in their wake were the more adventurous of the fashionable travel set, for whom the eastern resort circuits had become somewhat staid. Their curiosity piqued by the glowing reports of King and Bowles, they came to the Yosemite to experience for themselves the grandeur and uniqueness of what was being touted as the most romantically sublime landscape in America, if not the entire world. Culturally they came equipped with the landscape tastes and travel habits fashionable among their class. That they were to perceive and utilize Yosemite within this context was not only understandable but to be expected. Throughout the 1870s and 1880s Yosemite was perceived as a fashionable pleasure resort with all the philosophical trappings that such designation implied. In the midst of Yosemite's extraordinary natural scenery contemporary travelers sought to impose upon the landscape tastes, habits, and artifacts that were traditional in both form and function.

The overwhelming impression upon visitors was the degree to which Yosemite scenery embodied the very essence of romantic nature, with emphasis upon the sublime. The face and majesty of God were seen in every cliff and waterfall. Phrases such as "solidified vastness," "infinity petrified," and "the very buttresses of eternity" filled the tourist literature as travelers sought to adjust their levels of comprehension and experience to the scarcely believable scale of the Yosemite landscape.

When their own descriptive vocabulary failed them visitors frequently resorted to comparisons to better-known scenic attractions in the East or Europe. These comparisons served not only to provide interested persons with a frame of reference but also reiterated the

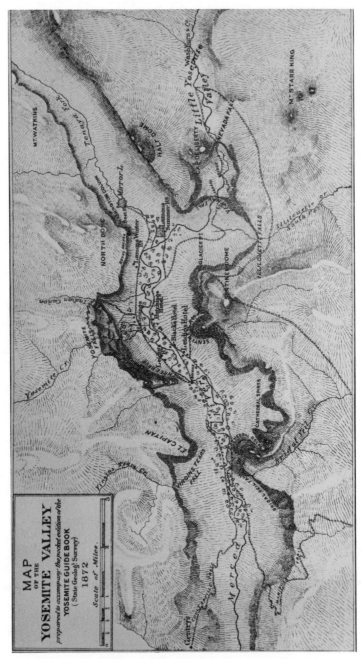

Figure 10. Yosemite Valley. From *The Yosemite Guide Book*, 1871.

popular contention that in America—at least, in Yosemite—romantic nature had achieved its loftiest expression. Starr King, for example, was happy to believe what travellers from Europe, from Sinai, "from the wildest passes of the Peruvian Andes," told him, that nowhere had they seen "such rocks and such waterfalls as those among which we had passed three glorious summer days."[1] An English gentleman, a member of the "celebrated Alpine Club," spent seventeen days in Yosemite, and upon leaving he remarked to James Hutchings that he had never left a place with so much pleasurable regret in all his life. "I have several times visited all the noted places in Europe, and many that are out of the ordinary tourist's round," he continued. "I have crossed the Andes in three different places, and been conducted to the sights considered most remarkable—I have been among the charming scenery of the Sandwich Islands, and the mountain districts of Australia, but never have I seen so much of sublime grandeur relieved by so much beauty, as that which I have witnessed in Yo-Semite."[2]

Perhaps the best way to convey the spirit of the romantic appreciation of Yosemite attractions is to sample the literary responses of contemporary visitors. Such responses often depended heavily upon the writings of early interpreters like Starr King or Josiah Whitney, the California state geologist whose definitive guide to the Yosemite constituted the most popular and oft-quoted reference work for several decades. Although criticized by later authors as being overly sentimental and verbose to the extreme, at the time these travel accounts were fashionable and appropriately romantic expressions of nature appreciation.

Common to most tourists' accounts was the pause at Inspiration Point, overlooking the Valley entrance from the south rim. There, for the first time, if one approached the Yosemite on the Wawona Trail, the grandeurs of Yosemite Valley were unfolded to the eye. The view was truly striking. Framed between the sheer, massive bulk of El Capitan on the left and the graceful Bridalveil Fall on the right, the Valley floor resembled a carefully-landscaped park, while off in the distance the brooding Half Dome hinted at even greater wonders in the distance. It was a view calculated to inspire the most insensitive of human souls. To the romanticist, whose emotional anticipation had already been whipped to a fever pitch, it was a sight which prompted one to wax rhapsodic:

> That name (Inspiration Point) had appeared pedantic, but we found it only the spontaneous expression of our own feelings on the spot. We did not so

much seem to be seeing from that crag of vision a new scene on the old familiar globe, as a new heaven and a new earth into which the creative spirit had just been breathed. I hesitate now, as I did then, at the attempt to give my vision utterance. Never were words so beggared for an abridged translation of any Scripture of Nature.[3]

In his own inimitable style Ludlow "hesitated" once more to give his "vision utterance" as he contemplated the Valley spread before him.

There lies a sweep of emerald grass turned to chrysoprase by the slant-beamed sun,—chrysoprase beautiful enough to have been the tenth foundation-stone of John's apocalyptic heaven. Broad and fair just beneath us, it narrows to a little strait of green between the butments that uplift the giant domes. Far to the westward, widening more and more, it opens into the bosom of great mountain ranges,—into a field of perfect light, misty by its own dying sun . . . Not a living creature, either man or beast, breaks the visible silence of this inmost paradise; but for ourselves, standing at the precipice, petrified, as it were, rock on rock, the great world might well be running back in stone-and-grassy dreams to the hour when God had given him as yet but two daughters, the crag and the clover.[4]

Figure 11. Yosemite Valley from Inspiration Point.

The view from Inspiration Point was perhaps the most purely romantic of any of the regularly visited Yosemite attractions. Few fashionable travelers were able to withstand its poetic appeal. It will be remembered that it was from this viewpoint that Samuel Bowles, a normally temperate Massachusetts newspaper editor, experienced "the confrontal of God face to face, as in great danger, in solemn, sudden death." Inspiration Point, El Capitan, Yosemite Falls, Half

Dome, the Giant Sequoia—these were the principal points which inspired comment from contemporary tourists.

There were times when visitors found that the reality of Yosemite failed to live up to their expectations. When introduced to the Grizzly Giant, in the Mariposa Grove of giant sequoia, Isaac Bromley confessed to being "dismally disappointed." After having prepared himself for the experience by "working up pretty carefully" what he should "probably think about them," supposing that he would be "inspired" to "soar on the wings of fancy, and all that sort of thing," he found that he "was not inspired at all." He couldn't think of anything that he wanted to "put down, except for lunch, and as for soaring, nothing in

Figure 12. Thomas Hill's romanticized perception of Yosemite Village.

the world could make me soar except my unfortunate horse, and he had done it already so that I could hardly turn in the saddle."[5]

For the majority of tourists, the Yosemite landscape more than lived up to its expectations; indeed, most would have agreed with Ralph Waldo Emerson that "this valley is the only place that comes up to the brag and exceeds it." Even Bromley repented of his initial reactions— or, rather, the lack thereof—and succumbed to his romantic inclinations as follows:

> Sitting there by the side of this prone Monarch ... the idea of its vastness took full possession of me, and for the first time I grasped its greatness. And even then I do not think the idea of size and measurement so overwhelmed me as did the thought of its vast age and the centuries it had looked down upon ... No inanimate monument of man's work was here—no unwrapping

31

of dead Pharaohs from the mummy-cloths of the embalmers; but here had been life and growth and increase in figures that could not be mistaken from the heart of the sapling out to the last rind of bark that hugged its age. And though one looks with profoundest wonder at the vast size of these monsters, it is, after all, the suggestion they give of their far reach backward into time that most impresses the beholder.[6]

That Bromley should make reference to the mummy cloth of dead pharaohs was a typically romantic comparison, and illustrated once again the propensity of contemporary tourists to incorporate romantic associations into their perceptions of natural scenery. Romanticists

Figure 13. Big Trees, Mariposa Grove. From *Picturesque America*, 1872.

found many such opportunities in the Yosemite landscape. References to the monumental structures of ancient Greece and Rome were common in the comments of visitors as they contemplated the giant cliffs and domes of the Yosemite Sierra. To many the quiet tranquility of the Valley floor, with its stately oaks and gentle wanderings of the Merced River, was reminiscent of an ancient cathedral that called one forth to worship. Such a reaction was a particularly popular response of visitors to the Mariposa Grove of big trees and is illustrated by the experience of a now thoroughly repentant Bromley in a thoroughly romantic mode:

> We spent three or four hours in the two groves, upper and lower—and just in the edge of the Sabbath twilight, singing in full chorus, "Praise God from whom all blessings flow," passed out from among the unhewn columns and sturdy pillars, the groined arches and leafy aisles, the heights and depths, and vistas and recesses, the grandeur and the solitude of these noblest of "God's first temples," and took up our journey towards the valley.[7]

A traditional component of the middle-nineteenth century pleasure resort was emphasis upon the restoration of health. That this notion was part of the contemporary perception of Yosemite was repeatedly affirmed by both management officials and visitors. Indeed, in the minds of the Yosemite Valley commissioners, the "salubrity of the atmosphere," along with the Valley's "scenic effects," encompassed "the two attractions of the region."[8] In their attempts to enhance the "attractiveness of the region as a resort for health and pleasure," the commissioners sought diligently to procure funds from the state legislature in order to "offer every inducement for a prolonged stay to those who visit us as tourists, whether in search of health or of the picturesque and grand in nature."[9] As early as 1857 the valley was "resorted to" by invalids and persons suffering from the intense summer heat of lower elevations. According to the commissioners, during the summer of 1875 a party of twenty-two persons spent three weeks in the Yosemite. With them were a lady and a child, the latter only three months old, both of whom supposedly were dying when they left Mariposa. After an absence from home of only six weeks, they had returned "in good health and vigorous condition."[10]

Foremost among Yosemite health "success" stories, however, was that of Galen Clark, perhaps the most popular and respected of the Yosemite Valley commissioners. Financial difficulties and ill health had prompted his move west in 1853. At about the time he established his homestead in the Wawona area he recorded suffering from "a severe attack of hemorrhage of the lungs from which I was given up to die at any hour."[11] As it turned out, life in the Sierra produced a remarkable change in his constitution; he spent the next fifty years in the Yosemite in his various capacities as innkeeper, guide, interpreter, guardian, and friend to apparently all who knew him.

Another expression of the commissioners' perception of Yosemite as a health resort consisted of their recommendation to develop on Tenayah Creek a "strong chalybeate spring," which Dr. T. R. Lees, the "eminent English chemist, pronounced the finest he had ever seen."[12] Partaking of the waters of such mineral springs had been a traditional feature of fashionable resort life for more than a century. The desire to develop such a spring in Yosemite was but further confirmation of the area's perceived function as a contemporary health and pleasure resort.

One of the principal characteristics of fashionable nineteenth century pleasure travel was the highly developed social consciousness of its participants. This was particularly true in post-Civil War America, with the emergence of a newly wealthy class of merchants, industrialists, and transportation moguls. Eager to be included as part of "society" and partakers of the "good life" as defined therein, aspirants diligently sought to ape the manners, tastes, and habits of what was generally considered fashionable society. In this respect the Yosemite tourist of the 1860s, 1870s, and 1880s was typical of his times. While it is doubtful that many of the Atlantic seaboard's most fashionable elite strayed so far from Newport as the Pacific coast and Yosemite, it is, nevertheless, important to realize that their influence and standards of behavior were felt wherever Americans endowed with the means and inclinations to travel chose to go. As far as the perception and utilization of Yosemite were concerned, what mattered was not so much the precise social status of visitors but their intentions and behavior. In this respect the Yosemite visitor of the several decades following the Civil War was keenly conscious of the perceptual, social, and habitual manifestations of contemporary fashionable travel.

One of the most pervasive characteristics of such travel was the propensity of tourists to follow the carefully prescribed itineraries laid out in guidebooks. These itineraries more or less demanded visits to those areas designated by fashion leaders as noteworthy for either their scenic or curiosity qualities. In return, writers of tourist guidebooks sought eagerly to attract the interest and patronage of fashionable travelers. Samuel Kneeland, for example, in his 1872 book titled *The Wonders of Yosemite Valley and of California*, dedicated his book specifi-

Figure 14. "The Yo-Semite Waterfall." From *Scenes of Wonder and Curiosity*, 1871.

cally to "the crowd of pleasure-seekers who make their annual visitations to Niagara, Newport, Saratoga, Cape May, and other centers of fashion, frivolity, foppery, and folly."[13]

Upon their arrival at Yosemite, tourists' itineraries followed more or less established patterns. While this was due in part to the recommendations and schedules of the guide service available, it was likewise true that visitors were anxious to experience for themselves the wonders described and sanctioned in the travel literature. Day excursions to the Valley's principal attractions were made on horseback at first, and included visits to the foot of Yosemite Falls, which prompted numerous comparisons with European, specifically Swiss, waterfalls of inevitably inferior dimensions, and Bridalveil Fall, with its mysterious Indian associations. Enroute visitors passed among lush meadows punctuated by irregularly spaced oak trees, reminiscent "of the beautiful parks of Europe, especially those of England and France." High overhead loomed the massive bulk of El Capitan, Sentinel Rock, Half Dome, and other recognized features of the surrounding granite walls. A "must" for the truly romantic tourist was a morning sojourn to Mirror Lake, where the elegant profile of Mt. Watkins achieved mirror-like reflection on the placid waters below. On a more rigorous level, but still considered de rigueur, was the ride up what was then sometimes called the "South Fork Canyon" to Vernal and Nevada falls. Particularly thrilling was the ascent of the wooden ladders that led adventurous tourists up through the mist and spray to the top of Vernal Fall. For the still hardier tourist a trail led from the Valley floor to Glacier Point, from which the superlative views of the Valley region, its surrounding walls, and the High Sierra to the east were surpassed only by the magnitude of Half Dome's sheer expanse of granite cliff. Less vigorous tourists could enjoy the vista from Glacier Point by taking the longer but more secure route which led to the point from the south via the Wawona trail. For the most part, however, tourists restricted their wanderings to the Valley floor and those areas that could be reached in the comfort of a carriage, when such became available.

At a time when Americans were exuberantly celebrating democracy's first century of existence the fashionable pleasure traveler persisted in his efforts to maintain Old World social and perceptual values. In his choice of travel companions, travel conditions, and destinations he was remarkably untainted by the spirit and purposes of democracy. Rather, he sought to maintain traditional class stratification in his travel experience and avoided where possible circumstances and persons considered undesirable by his own definitions of social propriety. Western establishments catering to fashionable travel recognized these preferences and advertised accordingly. "Members of our excursion parties form a select company, and are relieved of the annoyance of being placed in proximity to strangers, and, as it often happens in ordinary traveling, undesirable people."[14] An 1884 railroad advertisement cited the relatively high cost of western travel as an effective social discriminator when it suggested that cheap fares to the Atlantic resorts meant that they no longer had a homogeneous society of well-bred and cultured people, whereas expense, among other factors, insured the company of wealthy and cultured Englishmen and

Easterners in Colorado.[15] This form of elitism was as prevalent in Yosemite as in Colorado, and colored most aspects of the contemporary visitor experience.

Fashionable Yosemite tourists maintained well-defined social barriers between themselves and local folk. Landlords, guides, and other "service personnel" were treated much as titled Europeans were imagined to treat the servant classes in travel abroad. Such overt class distinctions and snobbery were resented by "non-fashionables" in Yosemite and often were the basis of the sharp philosophical and management differences that came to characterize the latter years of the nineteenth century. Landlords were regarded somewhat more highly than other service personnel, due no doubt to the strength of personality of such individuals as James Hutchings and Galen Clark. Hutchings, in particular, was more the congenial host than the subser-

Figure 15. El Capitan. From *California: For Health, Pleasure, and Residence*, 1893.

vient landlord, and in his own flamboyant way added significantly to the dimensions of a contemporary Yosemite experience.

Less-gifted innkeepers were rather more tolerated than appreciated and it was only with surprise that fashionable travelers discovered that the "natives," in their rough way, could also be sensitive to the beauties of Yosemite. In this respect, Starr King seems to have derived a great deal of amusement from his landlord Peck and quoted several of Mr. Peck's descriptions of Yosemite phenomena in his letters to the *Transcript*. In describing a Valley thunderstorm, Peck is quoted as saying "Jerusalem! How the fire flew, and how the thunder did butt that cliff! It was a great fight. Every now and then, the fog would kinder back off, to let the thunder see whether the rock was down, and then it would close in and let fly again. I tell ye now, the champion fight between Europe and Ameriky was nothin' to it!" Later, in describing the after effects of a spring storm in his "local" dialect, "the streams come slipping down them steep stripes, and I tell ye it's beautiful, jest like calico!"[16]

If fashionable tourists were condescending in their relationships with their hosts, and sometimes imperious in their attitudes toward guides and other hired help, they were often scathingly racist in their reactions to the Indian populations of Yosemite. In his highly regarded and authoritative guidebook, Whitney reported that the number of Indians actually and permanently resident in and about the Yosemite or the Mariposa Grove was very small. "Like the rest of the so-called 'diggers' in California," he wrote, "they are a miserable, degraded, and fast-disappearing set of beings, who must die out before the progress of the white man's civilization, and for whom there is neither hope nor chance."[17] Olive Logan, a female visitor who admittedly was not the most unbiased of contemporary visitors, described her perceptions of Yosemite's Indians as follows:

> There is an Indian camp beside Hutchings'. It looks romantic from this point. Let us get nearer. A vile stench greets us. These filthy wretches found a dead horse yesterday, and are now eating some of its carcass . . . It will not do to approach these people too closely; they are covered with vermin. Their copper skins are black as soot in spots; this is caked dirt, pure and simple. They are clad in the discarded tatters of civilization; and how tattered the discarded garment of the Sierra Nevada mountaineer is, no one can know who has not seen. The consequence is that the sight of these people so near a pleasure resort is an offence to decency. They glare at us as we approach. It is easy to see that these people (although Ferguson assured us they were "tame") would have no humanitarian scruples about waging a war of extermination against the whites if they had but the power.[18]

Although few guests would have gone to the extremes of Miss Logan, in spirit they would have sympathized with her perceptions of Yosemite's Indians as less decorative than colorful, more detractive than attractive. Contemporary romanticists appreciated their "noble savages" more in the abstract than in the flesh, and while they often were entranced by romantic associations of landscape with aboriginal life, they preferred their contact with American Indians to be on a literary level rather than on a face to face basis. Even Hutchings, despite his efforts to romanticize and popularize Indian lore in

Figure 16. Indians in Yosemite Valley, 1887.

Yosemite, was content to restrict his relationships with contemporary Indians to those of a manager to his hired laborers. Not until a later generation did the Indian become an object of visitor interest, and then more as a museum attraction than as a fellow human occupant.

Further insight into the perception and utilization of the Yosemite landscape can be obtained by analyzing the various ways that visitors chose to spend their time there. In general the romantic tourist was inclined to enjoy nature in an intellectual and/or artistic mode. With some exceptions, the physically active and more rigorous outdoorsman type would characterize a later generation of nature enthusiasts. The typically romantic tourist was more likely to respond to a particularly scenic view by quoting from one of the great romantic poets, or, like Starr King, prolonging a pleasurable sensation by engaging in a moment of quiet meditation. Lying alone at the foot of a giant sequoia, King watched the "golden sunshine mounting the amber trunk, and at last leaving a hundred feet of it in shadow to flood its mighty boughs and locks with tender lustre. What silence and what mystery!"[19] Charles Stoddard wrote of an early autumn visit to Yosemite in 1869 of the "long, stinging nights, plenty of woolen blankets, and delicious sleep. Then the evenings, so cosy around the fire. H———— reads Scott; we listen and comment."[20]

The middle nineteenth century passion for natural science found expression in a variety of amateur activities. It was fashionable to refer to works of famous naturalists and to collect specimens ranging from pressed flowers and butterflies to seashells and fossils. Less acquisitive

Figure 17. Gilded Age Tourists at Yosemite Falls. From *Man and Yosemite*, ca. 1880.

and more artistic romanticists preferred the sketch pad to the specimen box; indeed, a favorite pastime in Yosemite or any other notable resort was to accumulate a portfolio of drawings made at particularly romantic settings. Fitz Hugh Ludlow's tourist party, although a little out of the ordinary due to the presence of well-known artist Albert Bierstadt, consisted of "artists with their camp-stools and color-boxes, sages with their goggles, nets, botany-boxes, and bug-holders, and gentlemen of elegant leisure with their naked eyes and a fish-rod or a gun."[21]

As a fashionable pleasure resort Yosemite undoubtedly attracted a certain number of travelers who were less interested in Yosemite as a scenic wonder than they were in frequenting what had become virtually a social requirement of a trip to the far west. Such visitors, it was claimed, tended to frequent fashionable resorts "not to worship nature, but to see and be seen by their kind. They play tennis and golf, swim in warmed tanks, drive behind fine horses, dress for dinner, and do all these things in the conventional and polite way."[22] Woefully out of element in the Yosemite environment, it was this type of tourist who prompted the observation by a visiting Englishman that "American ladies never walk, but they go out 'buggy-riding' in dancing shoes and ball dresses, or amble about on ponies in highly ornamental riding habits. All this seems very odd among the mountains."[23]

Figure 18. An appropriately romantic pastime.

The majority of Yosemite's high fashion visitors were usually content to spend the bulk of their Yosemite time exchanging impressions with other tourists on the hotel verandas or reading "Scott" around the fireplace. When they did venture out to perform their obeisance to the ritual gods of Yosemite tourism, they rejoiced that, as one traveler put it, "all the celebrated features of Yosemite can be enjoyed from a carriage."[24] Only when necessary did such tourists resort to the considerably greater discomfort of horse trails. When they did so their habits were repulsive to John Muir, who scorned their "blank, fleshly apathy" in the face of nature. "They climb sprawlingly to their saddles like overgrown frogs pulling themselves up a streambank through the bent sedges, ride up the valley with about as much emotion as the horses they ride upon, and comfortable when they have 'done it all,' long for the safety and flatness of their proper homes." Muir thought it fortunate that most of them floated "slowly about the bottom of the valley as a harmless scum, collecting in hotel and saloon eddies, leaving the rocks and falls eloquent as ever and instinct with imperishable beauty and greatness."[25]

The trouble with Muir was that his biases were not in harmony with traditional tourist philosophies. To the contemporary traveler the enjoyment of nature was more emotional and intellectual than physical;

scenery was not to be "groveled in" but rather to be sensed and contemplated. In this respect, the "hotel and saloon eddies," with their tradition of after-hours reading, writing, and conversation, functioned as an integral component of contemporary tourism. Indeed, the resort hotel was both focus and setting for much of what constituted fashionable pleasure travel. As a French traveler who visited the United States in 1887 observed, "in Europe the hotel is a means to an end. In America it is the end . . . Hotels are for (the American) what cathedrals, monuments and the beauties of nature are for us."[26]

Whereas in the case of Yosemite this was something of an overstatement, the hotel was, nevertheless, a tourist attraction in its own right. Early Yosemite innkeepers, especially James Hutchings, were well aware of this fact and did whatever they could to encourage it. Throughout his writings and guidebooks Hutchings seldom missed an

Figure 19. J. M. Hutchings and party.

opportunity to "put in a plug" for hotels in general and his own in particular. "Hutchings', in Yosemite," was always the end point in any of his discussions on how to get to Yosemite and what to do while there. In his popular 1870 guidebook *Scenes of Wonder and Curiosity in California* he stressed that after the long, hot, dusty ride to the Valley, "you will begin to feel that a refreshing glass of good California wine, a bath, dinner, and such other acceptable comforts as may be found at Hutchings' are not to be despised." Farther on in the same book, as he leads another hypothetical tourist group to the end of a long day's trail, filled as it was with awe and exclamations at the wonders they had seen, he rejoices that "one ejaculation that seems to contain more real satisfaction in it than any amount of sightseeing just now is this one: 'Thank goodness. Here's the Yo-Semite Hotel. Here's Hutchings'!'—

and commending ourselves to its most generous hospitalities—for we need them—we will dismount in the hope that a refreshing glass of pure California wine, a good wash, and an acceptable dinner await us."[27]

Contrary to Hutchings' wishful illusions, Yosemite hotels were a far cry from normal tourist-attraction hotels such as the Del Monte in Monterey or the Raymond in Pasadena. Seldom more than a barracks-type structure of simple, wooden frame construction, they were likely to be equipped with nothing more than muslin sheets with which to divide sleeping chambers. Tolerantly amused by these primitive conditions at first, Yosemite visitors soon tired of "local color" and began clamoring to the California state legislature, which controlled the Yosemite, for better accommodations. The one exception to this pattern was J. C. Smith's Cosmopolitan House, enthusiastically described by a contemporary traveler as containing a saloon, billiard hall, bathing

Figure 20. Leidig's Hotel.

rooms, barber shop, mirrors full-length, pyramids of elaborate glassware, costly service, the finest of cues and tables, reading-room handsomely furnished and supplied with the latest from Eastern cities, and baths with "unexceptional surroundings." In its essential characteristics, the Cosmopolitan resembled closely the casinos at the fashionable Atlantic coast seaside resorts of Newport and Narragansett Pier, Rhode Island. According to Yosemite's foremost historian, Dr. Carl P. Russell,

> To say that J. C. Smith figured in early Yosemite affairs is hardly expressive. His baths, his drinks, and the various unexpected comforts provided by his Cosmopolitan left lasting impressions that vied with El Capitan when it came to securing space in books written by visitors. The ladies exclaimed over the cleanliness of the bathtubs; a profusion of towels, fine and coarse;

Figure 21. Cosmopolitan Bath House and Saloon, 1870s.

delicate toilet soaps, bay rum, Florida water, arnica, court plaster; needles, thread, and buttons; and late copies of the *Alta* and the *Bulletin* for fresh "bustles." The men found joy in "a running accompaniment of 'brandy-cock-tails,' 'gin-slings,' 'barber's poles,' 'eye-openers,' 'mint-julep,' 'Sampson with the hair on,' 'corpse-revivers,' 'rattle-snakes,' and other potent combina-tions."[28]

The normal length of stay for a Yosemite visit was three to four days, in spite of the distance and difficulty met in such a trip. Had Mr. Smith's Cosmopolitan House been able to accommodate overnight as many guests as it served during the day, the length of stay might well have been three to four weeks, as was commonly the case in luxurious resort hotels of the Del Monte class. The Cosmopolitan was for many years the only establishment in Yosemite in which a fashionable nineteenth century tourist could feel at home and take pleasure in patronizing. Not until the late 1880s, when the state-built Stoneman House was com-pleted, were there facilities in Yosemite which could cater to the wants and tastes of contemporary tourists as could the Cosmopolitan. Hotels there were, but anything more than an unsatisfactory bed and plain food they were not.

The cry for more "commodious" accommodations was not the only call for improvements that fell regularly upon the ears of the Yosemite Valley commissioners. Travel conditions, in particular, came regularly under condemnation by the more exacting, less-hardy tourist who was beginning to frequent the Yosemite in increasing numbers. That the Yosemite was truly a land of wonders few cared to deny. It could neither be denied that some of the most remarkable of these wonders were encountered enroute in the form of physical discomfort. According to one traveler, "the comfort of passengers is just the last thing considered on the Yosemite journey." The ever-eloquent Olive Logan complained of being "dirty, sick, sore, and miserable, and at night, as we creep heartsick to bed, we can think of nothing but—the Yo Semite Fall, the Bridal Veil, El Capitan, the Cathedral Rocks? No! Of the weary distance which lies between us and civilization."[29] Existing roads were poor, slow, and covered deeply with a fine dust which bestowed itself upon the hot, uncomfortable passengers of the stages in prodigious amounts.

> The road, to draw it very mild, was dusty. We had been told it would be. But dust was no name for it. The heavy teams of the ranch-men had cut it up and ground and pulverized it to a condition of volatility fearful to contemplate, and our stage sunk into it to the hubs, while it rose up and enveloped us. The wind followed us, and there was no such thing as getting ahead of the clouds; nothing to do but chew it and sneeze, and try to get used to it, and accept the consolation of the driver that coming back it would be ever so comfortable, because the wind would be in our faces and the dust be blown behind. The amount of real estate we took up was almost incredible.[30]

Beyond the roads the tourist was subjected to long hours in the saddle, an experience for which most were physically unprepared. Accommodations between Stockton and Yosemite were primitive and amounted to little more than trail-side boarding houses which were

Figure 22. Stagecoach trailing dust cloud.

located far too infrequently for comfortable scheduling. In spite of her great enthusiasm for the beauties of Yosemite itself, the Lady C. F. Gordon-Cumming decried the travel conditions to and from the Valley. "Just imagine those people in San Francisco telling us that we could see the Valley ("do" the Valley is the correct expression) in two days, but that three would be ample!" she wrote reproachfully. "Three days of jolting over the roughest roads—three days of hard work rushing from point to point in this wonderland, and then the weary journey to be done over again, shaking all impressions of calm beauty from our exhausted minds."31

Another tourist of the gentle sex, who was, to put it mildly, something less than impressed by her Yosemite tour, wrote scathingly about the horrid conditions to which she was subjected in her delightfully candid article "Does It Pay To Visit Yo Semite?" In her opinion it most decidedly did not, and she devoted a great deal of energy to caustically condemning tourist conditions both enroute and within Yosemite Valley. She furthermore concluded that only "lunatics . . . very low down indeed in the depths of imbecility" would knowingly risk the hardships of a Yosemite tour, "and the plain truth is that nine out of ten who visit Yo Semite think this, but they will not say what they think."32 The rigors and hardships of a Yosemite tour were not without their merits. Certainly they were very much a part of the contemporary Yosemite experience. Furthermore, in many cases they seemed to add a great deal of color and a certain degree of charm to a Western tour.

> All these little inconveniences, to which they (the tourists) may be subjected here, will, on their arrival home, turn into sources of pleasure. They shall then boast to their friends how they roughed it; how they slept in blankets; how they rode up and down those eternal hills on mustangs, branded and vented, with Mexican saddles and big wooden stirrups. And also, with little thrills of pride and pleasure, they will deal out bits of the California vernacular, and talk knowingly about ranches, corrals, canons, camps, plazas, and presidios.33

In response to the demands of dissatisfied tourists, facilities improved continually—if slowly—both within Yosemite and in areas utilized in the approach thereto. Each year the railroad crept closer to the Valley floor. Roads were built, improved, and sprinkled to minimize dust and other discomforts. By the season of 1875 three roads were completed to the floor of Yosemite Valley. Within the Valley itself accommodations increased in quantity and quality. New hotels were built and old ones renovated or razed. Boardwalks were constructed between them in order that guests who chose to do a little walking might do so unsullied by the dust of summer and the mud of spring and autumn. Other than the Cosmopolitan House, however, these did not meet the standards of the tourists. Consequently, in 1886, the state of California constructed a multi-story frame hotel called the Stoneman House. Plagued from the start by construction difficulties and damage from unusually heavy winter snows, the Stoneman House was in constant need of renovation until its destruction by fire in 1896. By that time tourist fashions and the nature of the tourist himself had changed

Figure 23. The Stoneman House, Yosemite Valley.

to the extent that Yosemite Valley's next luxury hotel did not appear on the scene until 1927 when the lush Ahwahnee was opened for business. The demand for luxury accommodations that continued to exist in the interim was met, more or less, by the railroad-built hotel at El Portal, approximately ten miles from the Valley.

The majority of Yosemite's tourists hailed from the American northeast and represented distinctly upper social and economic standing in their respective communities. Another 15 percent or so were foreigners, mainly from the British Isles, and represented both titled nobility and adventurous representatives of the leisure classes. From the beginning, however, there was another group of tourists frequenting the "Incomparable Valley." Generally less-affluent, more physically adventurous, and of lesser social status, these individuals were less fashionably romantic in their perception and enjoyment of the Yosemite country. Most were Californians; by the early 1880s almost one-third of Yosemite's visitors originated from within the borders of the Golden State. Although in some cases these visitors attempted anxiously to fit into fashionable tourist modes, in many others they were less than adulatory, even to the point of being highly critical, of the romantic and fashionable travel society that still dominated Yosemite tourism. For example, the tendency to wax rhapsodic over a particularly scenic feature was a common source of amusement to the more pragmatically inclined westerner. Even Clarence King, a native Newporter who fell into Western ways with an ease that belied his birth, poked fun at the literary inclinations of his contemporaries who felt compelled to record for posterity their impressions of Inspiration Point. "Here all who make California books, down to the last and most sentimental specimen who so much as meditates a letter to his or her local newspaper, dismounts and inflates."[34]

To many of this hardier breed of tourist the propensity of fashionable travelers to adhere to established itineraries suggested less a concern for the beauties of nature than a compulsion to meet all the requirements of a domestic "Grand Tour." "Americans often seem to travel for the mere satisfaction of going through a new country, and staying the night in a new hotel. They add them to their collection, so to say, as an entomologist adds a beetle."[35] Visiting Yellowstone around the turn of the century, Ray Stannard Baker observed that most of the tourists remained "pretty snuggly" in their coach-seats or near the hotels. They were often seen in great loads, some wrapped in long linen coats, some wearing black glasses, some broad, green-brimmed hats. "Occasionally one sees them devouring their guidebooks and checking off the sights as they whirl by, so that they will be sure not to miss anything or see anything twice." One old gentleman, accompanied by his stenographer, after each excursion sat on the piazza, guidebook in hand, and dictated an account of what he had seen.[36]

In a rather scathing commentary on eastern tourists visiting Yosemite in the early 1870s, Prentice Mulford wrote that sometimes "the East" stayed in the valley but a day. There came men and women, content to ride in, sup, sleep, breakfast, glance at the falls and cliffs, and then ride straight out again. For them, the valley "was done, and they thanked heaven that they had done it. It was not to be visited again; and that epoch of a restless, weary life in search of pleasure was over." Mulford was incensed at visitors whose insensitivity allowed them to "take in" Yosemite's wonders in a single day. At the same time he could sympathize with persons whose life experience had totally failed to prepare them for the immensity that was Yosemite. "A soul cluttered up for years in a press of pork, flour, codfish, fashion, household and worldly cares, requires some little time ere it expands proportionate to Yosemite's grandeur."[37]

While Californians were as often amused as offended by the "antics" of fashionable eastern travelers, some became increasingly denunciatory in their criticism of the Yosemite Valley Commission. The state-appointed commissioners were essentially traditionalists in their attitudes toward nature and, as such, were decidedly more in sympathy with fashionable romanticists and the financial return they represented than they were in the concerns of the local citizenry. Spearheaded by John Muir and his sympathizers, critics decried such commission policies as fencing and cultivating the Valley meadows for pasturage and the cutting of trees for a variety of purposes, including the betterment of scenic views from the veranda of a resort hotel. A highly censorious editorial appeared in an 1889 issue of *Garden and Forest* magazine which rejoiced that "the press of California is at last thoroughly aroused to the importance of reorganizing the board of Yosemite commissioners, who, if all the stories told about them are true, are about as undesirable a body of officials as can be found in California or any other state."[38] The editorial goes on to specify some of the charges being directed toward the commission.

> It was clearly the duty of the commissioners to preserve the natural scenery of the valley entrusted in their care; but instead of doing this, they have leased out all its level parts to a firm of contractors for a nominal price, and have allowed them to convert it into a hay farm, and to acquire a monopoly of all the forage sold in the valley. No visitor can now enter the valley on horseback or in a carriage without being compelled to pay an exorbitant tax to these contractors in the shape of the price demanded for the feed for his animals, while all visitors are subjected to unauthorized extortions imposed by the Commissioners or by their agents. The noble Black Oaks and Pines which once dotted the park-like valley or lined the banks of the Merced, where it flowed through charming natural meadows, have been cut down or trimmed up in order to increase the area of arable land; and the wild flowers, the natural grasses, the clumps of wild Roses and other native shrubs have all been grubbed up.
>
> The valley is everywhere intersected by barbedwire fences, closing the paths which lead across its undulated surface and shutting up many of the best points of view of the surrounding mountains. All freedom of enjoyment is ended, and all sense of naturalness destroyed. The grandeur of the mountains and the beauty of the mountain torrents the Commissioners have not yet been able to destroy, but the value of these even is lessened when

Figure 24. Degnan's Dairy Herd, Yosemite Valley.

seen across fields bounded by barbed-wire fences and torn up by a patent gang-plow.[39]

Stung by what they felt to be "the most amazing falsehoods that have ever been strung together upon such a subject" the commissioners responded by offering a series of letters written by recent visitors to the Valley, giving their impressions of its condition and management.[40] In both tone and substance these letters illustrate much by way of contemporary visitor perception and utilization of natural scenery. One of the harshest criticisms directed toward the commission was its policy of tree and brush removal. Partly with the goal in mind of restoring the meadows that, when protected from the ravages of fire, were being invaded by young trees, the commissioners sought to maintain the open park-like environment that had been one of the Yosemite's earliest attractions. That some visitors, at least, agreed with these attempts was indicated by the opinion of one visitor who felt that "the underbrush in the valley should be thoroughly cleaned out so as to give the impression of a park as much as possible." Another visitor went so far as to suggest that the commission should "cut away more of the trees and shrubs, and give the Valley a more park-like appearance—it could be made a beautiful park." The presence of buildings, fenced gardens and pastures, and other visible evidences of human occupation occasioned few comments from the majority of contemporary visitors. At least one tourist felt that "this touch of rural utilitarianism does not detract from the wild beauty of the surroundings." Rather, in the words of another visitor, "I think that a few of the evidences of civilization do not spoil the valley at all. It only adds to the picturesqueness"—a typically romantic evaluation.

For the most part, tourists then, as now, were seldom sympathetic to or knowledgeable about such day-to-day management concerns as fire protection, maintenance and clean-up, visitor accommodations, and access roads to scenic points. Particularly challenging was the need to provide food, fuel, construction supplies, and forage for livestock at an acceptable, if not totally reasonable, cost to an area that was, even by nineteenth century standards, geographically remote. That the commission was at least partly successful in their endeavors was acknowledged by a visitor who believed that a summer vacation could be spent at the Yosemite with as little expense as at any other resort on the coast, "a very wonderful improvement, indeed, and one that will make it possible for 'the people' to enjoy the grouped grandeur of this wonderland as they could not else."[41]

Regarding what he felt to be the generally satisfactory management of the Yosemite grant, a member of the California Senate judged the Yosemite Valley Commission to be "entirely competent." "It is comprised for the most part of gentlemen of taste, and several of the commissioners are persons who are ardently attached to the particular business incident to their office. I am satisfied that they do their duty faithfully." The senator went on to relate that

> While in the valley, I discussed many of the subjects which I have mentioned with intelligent tourists who have traveled over the greater portion of the globe sight-seeing, and none of them made as much criticism as is contained in what I have written. I learned, by means of the investigation of which I have before spoken, that there was a great deal of fuss made about nothing, and you undoubtedly know that a busybody with newspaper influence behind him can make much noise. A personal inspection of the valley is the best answer to the charges made against the Commissioners.[42]

At the heart of the controversy between the Yosemite Valley Commission and its critics was the reluctance of the traditionally conservative commissioners to adapt to changing trends in tourist fashions. Despite the fact that by the 1890s romanticism was slipping out of vogue among fashionable European and Eastern travelers, in the Yosemite change was slow in coming. Several examples can be used to illustrate the growing philosophical schism that divided Yosemite visitors. One of the most popular and traditionally romantic of Yosemite's attractions was Mirror Lake. Especially during the morning

Figure 25. Mirror Lake, Yosemite Valley. From *Picturesque America*, 1872.

hours, the mirror-like reflections of Mount Watkins in the tranquil waters of the lake provided an experience that was considered intensely romantic. Over the years a summer house, dance floor, and saloon were built on a platform that protruded out over the water. During the 1880s, when sediment transported by streams descending from the High Sierra threatened to fill in the lake, several dams were constructed to raise the level of the water. Any concern for modifying nature's handiwork or creating an artificial attraction was subsumed by the desire to maintain the lake's romantically esthetic attributes. Such "tampering" with natural processes was seen by some to border on sacrilege; commissioners, on the other hand, perceived such "improvement" as only appropriate to their duty.

Another "improvement" that was suggested by the commission had to do with the harnessing of the waterfalls for the production of electricity. A committee of the board considered introducing electric lights into the Valley, the dynamos for which to be run by the "ample hydraulic power" furnished by the various waterfalls. "This will add greatly to the attractions," felt the committee, "as it has to those of Niagara Falls, where electric light is in nightly use during the season." The committee maintained further that electric lights on the Yosemite trails and summits would enable effects "unrivaled in their awe-inspiring beauty, and serve to carry the fame of the valley farther than ever."[43]

Also recommended by the board was the mounting of an electric spotlight on the overlook at Glacier Point. The search light, it was felt, would be "novel and exceedingly attractive." When operated from Glacier Point it would be made to illuminate, in various colors, the Yosemite Falls, Vernal and Nevada falls, Mount Starr King, Cloud's Rest, and the various domes and cliffs. It could further be used to illuminate a fountain at night with its various "rainbow colors," and to produce "most novel night effects in Mirror Lake."[44] While such developments might have produced an apoplectic seizure in the likes of John Muir, to many a traditional romanticist, "the introduction of these improvements would be only keeping up with the times, and what would naturally be expected in a locality visited by so many people from all parts of the world."[45] Such an attitude was in keeping with the general philosophy of the commission: "Anything which adds to the accessibility of its (Yosemite's) features and to the comfort and satisfaction of the wonderseekers who resort to it is worthy the attention of this Board."[46]

By the latter years of the nineteenth century the traditionally romantic philosophy of the Yosemite Valley Commission was perceived by growing numbers of people as both outmoded and inappropriate. With the designation of the surrounding High Sierra as a national park in 1890, pressures mounted to recede the original Yosemite grant to the federal government for inclusion into the national park. Understandably, disgruntled commissioners resisted this movement, insisting that theirs was an administration that had complied with legislative directive insofar as the constraints imposed upon them by a penurious legislature had allowed. As to what manner of development and visitor utilization of Yosemite was more appropriate than another, a visitor stated the dilemma succinctly when he stated that "the citizens living in the valley, and the visitors to the valley, would never be united upon any one scheme of 'improvement,' either with ample or with insufficient means."[47] The governor of California, H. H. Markham, put it somewhat more diplomatically when he suggested that the subject simply involved a question of taste, "in which everyone will advocate his own particular aesthetical ideas, precisely as in the case of landscape gardening."[48]

With the close of the nineteenth century came the end of an era in Yosemite. For its first three decades as an internationally known tourist attraction, the Yosemite had functioned as an intensely romantic and fashionable pleasure resort. Despite the fact that romanticism, per se, had fallen somewhat from fashion among the traveling elite in Europe and the eastern United States, in Yosemite it persisted as the dominant philosophical perception of natural scenery. In Yosemite, under the management of the Yosemite Valley Commission, romanticism was expressed in countless ways as the commissioners sought to implement its elements both upon the landscape and the many aspects of the visitor experience.

Figure 26. A pastoral scene in Yosemite Valley.

Chapter 4
The Great Outdoors

THE COMPLETION OF THE STATE-BUILT Stoneman House in 1887 represented a major achievement for the Yosemite Valley Commission. Designed as a first-class hotel, the Stoneman House culminated a campaign of more than twenty years to provide suitable accommodations for the class of visitors the commissioners preferred to encourage. That it filled a void in existing facilities was evidenced by the fact that of the approximately 3,800 tourists that visited the Valley during the 1888 summer season, the Stoneman House accommodated more than half, while only a fourth stayed in the Valley's other hotel. Of utmost significance, however, were the remaining tourists, those who did not patronize either of the regular tourist hotels. Described by the commissioners as "campers," or "go as you please" tourists, this new class of visitor represented a more participative and aggressive style of landscape utilization. Outdoor recreation, i.e., camping, hiking, and fishing, was becoming increasingly popular at the relative, if not the absolute, expense of traditional romanticism. The hotel as an end point and tourist attraction in itself was rapidly being supplanted by the "Great Outdoors" as the popular way to enjoy the Yosemite. Campfires and trails were taking over the functions of verandas and roads as bases from which to experience the area's scenic attractions. When the Stoneman House met its destruction by fire in 1896, the fact that another luxury hotel was not built until thirty years later stands as mute testimony to the completeness of these changes. This was in spite of the fact that the annual number of Yosemite visitors increased seventy-fold during the same period.

Camping, as well as life in the outdoors in general, was certainly not new to the West; neither, for that matter, was it new to the Yosemite. People had camped in the Yosemite from the very first and had continued to do so through the years. As early as 1878 the commissioners had granted to a Mr. A. Harris the privilege of operating a public camping ground in the Valley east of the hotels. Nevertheless, camping as a means of touring the Yosemite was considered neither fashionable nor desirable by society-conscious travelers of the 1870s and 1880s, who generally looked with disdain upon the "vulgar" and "commonplace" class of people who were unable to afford the high costs of contemporary tourist accommodations.

Those who did choose to camp did not have an easy time of it. Aside from the difficulties of procuring necessary provisions in the Valley, campers found it next to impossible to obtain pasturage for their stock. What grasses were available in the meadows were as often as not fenced in and used exclusively by the commercial interests. Only by purchasing feed from them could the campers provide for their own animals. Moreover, the Yosemite Valley commissioners at first were of little help in furthering the campers' cause. Dominated by such men as J. S. Hutchings, the commission was decidedly in sympathy with traditional tourist custom, in which camping or any other form of "roughing it" had little place. Yet in spite of these obstacles the number of campers coming to Yosemite Valley grew steadily from an insignificant minority in the early years to a popular majority by the turn of the century. That they were able to do so was more an expression of changing national tourist patterns than a tribute to the persistence of the Californians who made up the bulk of these campers.

By the second half of the nineteenth century the attitudes of American philosophers toward nature were undergoing significant modification. Prompted by trends already popular in Europe, Americans were beginning to perceive their natural world less as a

Figure 27. Yosemite camping party, 1890.

medium for meditative appreciation than an arena in which to experience a more intensified and, by implication, a more satisfying association with nature. Growing out of the romantic propensity to emphasize the sublime in wild American landscapes, the "Wilderness Cult," as described by Roderick Nash in his *Wilderness and the American Mind* (1967), borrowed heavily from such transcendentalists as Thoreau and Emerson. In the face of an increasingly urban and imperfect society, it became popular to look "backward" to the simpler, more ordered world of "Mother Nature," wherein life proceeded according to "higher" principles.

By the last several decades of the nineteenth century it was becoming ever more apparent that industrialization was a mixed blessing. Whereas it was still possible to extol the virtues of prosperous farms and thriving cities, punctuated, as they were, by increasingly complex and gigantic marvels of modern engineering, it could not be denied that esthetically, at least, such developments left much to be desired. In an attempt to regain what had been "lost," Americans turned increasingly to nature as a source of inspiration and spiritual rejuvenation. According to Nash, the "Return to Nature" movement found expression in several related themes. The first of these was a growing tendency to associate wilderness with America's frontier epoch, around which had grown a mythology that suggested that much of what was peculiar and commendable about American culture could be attributed thereto. The second was related to the "Noble Savage" myth, i.e., that it was through direct confrontation with wilderness that human beings were

Figure 28. Joseph LeConte in camp, Yosemite.

imbued with virility, moral purity, and raw physical courage. The third theme lacked the "hairy-chestedness" of the previous ideas and instead recognized wild nature as a source of beauty and spiritual truth. Nash felt that Americans detected in the primitive those qualities of innocence, purity, cleanliness, and morality which seemed on the verge of succumbing to utilitarianism and the surge of progress. Furthermore, at a time when the force of religion "seemed vitiated by the new scientism on the one hand and social conflict on the other, wilderness acquired special significance as a resuscitator of faith."[1]

One of the ways in which Americans chose to become involved with nature was through the organization of outdoor clubs. Such clubs functioned primarily as social institutions in which one could become involved in all aspects of life in the great outdoors. Once again, the model was European. The British Alpine Club was the first, in 1857, and was followed by the Swiss in 1863, the French in 1874, the Appalachian Mountain Club in 1876, the Oregon Alpine Club in 1887, the Sierra Club in 1892, and the Mazamas in 1894. By the turn of the century the propensity of Americans to institutionalize nature activities expanded to include such youth organizations as Ernest Thompson Seton's Woodcraft Indians in 1902 and Daniel C. Beard's Sons of Daniel Boone and Boy Pioneers in 1905. Three years after its parent organization was established in England, the Boy Scouts of America was founded in 1910.

Accompanying the rise of nature organizations was the development of a new literary genre, the nature story. Although derided by some as "Nature Fakirs" because of their highly romantic and idealized anthropomorphism, writers such as Ernest Thompson Seton, Gene Stratton-Porter, Howard R. Garis, and Percy K. Fitzhugh nonetheless were extremely popular. Nature stories took on the aura of a peculiarly American morality play, in which the simplicity, honesty, and moral virtues of life in the great outdoors invariably triumphed over the complexity, sophistry, and evil of life in the city. Regardless of their literary qualities, such works probably influenced the attitudes of young Americans toward nature in a way unequalled by any other medium in a pre-television society. Periodical publications likewise developed nature themes and fostered serial fiction, poetry, and advice columns directed toward those interested in participating in outdoor life.

More important than the written word were the lessons that could be learned directly from nature. In this way the great outdoors enthusiast differed from his romanticist predecessors in that less emphasis was placed upon the works of well-known literary "lights" and more attention directed toward developing a personal relationship with nature. Such a relationship commonly assumed a reverential, religious tone; as Henry Wadsworth Longfellow wrote of his friend, the great naturalist Louis Agassiz,

> And Nature, the old nurse, took
> The child upon her knee,
> Saying, "Here is a story-book
> Thy Father has written for thee."[2]

Whether it was due to the propensity of westerners to look to the East for leadership in social conventions or, perhaps, because westerners were still so near in time to the way of life in which camping, hunting, and fishing were perceived as necessities rather than luxuries, the "back to nature" movement caught on somewhat later in the West. As Earl Pomeroy pointed out, easterners, following the lead of cultural innovators in Europe, had begun to discover nature well before the Civil War through Thoreau and his collaborators. Westerners, however, lagged behind their eastern counterparts in adopting the new attitudes toward nature. "While the paths by which Americans retreated to nature eventually were of all lengths and altitudes, at the beginning the least impressive were those that westerners built."[3] By the 1860s upper middle class westerners were beginning to venture forth in holiday camping expeditions into the Sierra Nevada, the Coast ranges, the Cascade Mountains of Oregon and Washington, and to various seaside locations along the Pacific coast. The style of these outdoor sojourns of the late 1860s and 1870s was a "charming blend of frontier and belle tournure. One roughed it by day and returned at evening to society and civilized surroundings."[4]

In California the presence of a growing and increasingly affluent population, along with a congenial physical environment, facilitated the popularization of the outdoors movement. Members of an emerging California "society," conscious of fashions popular along the Atlantic coast, were likewise desirous of partaking of activities and pleasures popular among fashionable social classes in the East. For whatever the reasons, Californians adopted the infatuation with the outdoors with enthusiasm and energy. In describing the numerous horse-drawn rigs which took to the road at the completion of the winter rainy season, a contemporary enthusiastically proclaimed the virtues of the "campers' state." For all alike, he wrote, the countryside was golden, the sun warm, the sky blue, the birds joyous, and the spring young in the land.

Figure 29. John Muir, 1907.

The climate was positively guaranteed. It would not rain; the sun would shine; the stars would watch. Feed for the horses abounded everywhere along the roads. "One can idle along the highways and the byways and the noways-at-all, utterly carefree, surrounded by wild and beautiful scenery. No wonder half the state turns nomadic in the spring."[5]

In the early years camping excursions to the more conveniently located seaside far outnumbered those to the more remote reaches of the Sierra Nevada. Early in the summer of 1868, however, a young Scotsman arrived at Yosemite Valley on foot who not only would help reverse that trend but would also change forever the ways in which Americans would perceive the natural landscape. With an Englishman as a companion, John Muir, a sometime inventor and machinist and always enthusiastic naturalist and traveler, began his auspicious career

Figure 30. John Muir and Theodore Roosevelt, Glacier Point, 1903.

as an interpreter, devotee, and champion of the Yosemite Sierra. For most of the ensuing half century Muir's life and ambitions were inextricably connected with Yosemite and the "Range of Light." Indeed, his associations have been such that to many persons interested in the development of wilderness philosophy and preservation in the United States, "John Muir and Yosemite are synonymous."[6]

It is difficult to assess objectively the contributions of John Muir as preservationist and interpreter-naturalist. On the one hand, many of his ideas merely echoed established tenets of transcendentalism, repeating with sometimes little variation the words of Thoreau. On the other hand, he demonstrated an ability to articulate his feelings with an intensity and enthusiasm that commanded widespread attention. Certainly during his later years, his alliance with and ability to influence such prominent personalities as Robert Underwood Johnson, editor of *The Century* magazine, and Theodore Roosevelt produced for him a degree of exaltation as a wilderness prophet unmatched in his time or since. Most certainly his career occurred at an auspicious moment in the development of perceptions and utilization of the natural landscape. As Roderick Nash put it, it was the context rather than the content of Muir's philosophies that determined his popularity.[7] Nevertheless, his uniquely rhapsodic and deeply imaginative responses to nature and, in particular, to the Yosemite earned for him the reputation as "the most magnificent enthusiast about nature in the United States, the most rapt of all prophets of our out-of-door gospel."[8] In his book *Americans and the California Dream, 1850–1915*, Kevin Starr offers an incisive analysis of Muir's character.

> Muir's relationship to nature could never be trivial. It filled the void left by an abandoned Calvinism and cured some of its scars. It also kept some of Calvinism's characteristics: a deep longing for communion as a pledge of redemption and a continual searching of the literal for symbols of salvation, an asceticism of means and ends in the pursuit of holiness, a capacity for prophecy and stewardship, and—most importantly—a sense of power, sacred and awful, at the core of creation. Schooled in classics and the Scriptures, Muir had language. Toughened by farm labor, he had endurance and a sinewy ability to get by on very little. It took California to consolidate Muir's aspirations and to give them expression and purpose, but they had their origins on a farm in the Wisconsin frontier.[9]

To John Muir, hiking and camping were but the means that allowed his physical person to become satiated with the sights, sounds, and smells that inspired his love affair with the "Range of Light." To his more prosaic disciples, hiking and camping were as much the essence of an experience in the outdoors as they were the means of getting there. From its modest beginnings early in Yosemite's tourist history, camping, by the 1880s and 1890s, had grown enormously in popular appeal. By the turn of the century it was pointed out by Foley's guidebook that "about two thousand campers (one-fourth of the annual visitors) come here in their own wagons and camp out. A good part of the Valley can be used by (them), permission first being granted from the office of the Acting Superintendent . . . The grounds are free." Campers pitched their tents practically everywhere in the Valley but concentrated mainly in the meadows east of the hotels where, according to Foley, it was not uncommon to see "five hundred laughing, joyous, noisy visitors" encamped there at any one time.[10] Californians made up the vast majority of this class of tourists, and with the change in popular prejudice toward the sport campers included persons from every social and financial class that was to be found in the Yosemite.

"Camping is the cheapest, most comfortable, most refreshing way of reaching this worshipful wonderland," wrote the Rev. Walter Laidlaw in 1897, and yet the sport of camping was still far from being an inexpensive proposition.[11] Aside from the amount of leisure time required for a trip to the Yosemite the cost of the equipment itself could be considerable. Furthermore, many of the campers of this period came accompanied by their own cooks and were sufficiently well off to remain in the Valley for weeks at a time. Often groups of friends or entire families would come to the Yosemite for extended campouts, the adults either relaxing, fishing, or otherwise "taking in" nature, while the younger set tramped about the Valley, swam in the brisk waters of the Merced, and generally enjoyed the freedom of the outdoors. Most of these large parties came from the cities and for many of them it became a family tradition to visit the Yosemite year after year in such a manner.

Camping truly had become the fashion; "everyone did it." Indicative of the change of attitude since the days of the hotel-bound romanticist were these "Impressions of a Careless Traveler" from the turn-of-the-century:

> I can hardly imagine a more delightful summer experience, than to go into the Yosemite Park with two or three congenial companions, get a competent and agreeable guide or two, and then spend four to six weeks traveling through these gorges, over these mountain ridges, in this primeval forest, camping at night, the fir boughs for a pillow, the sky for a roof, the trees and flowers and ferns for decorations, nature animate and inanimate for the interpreter, and God as the Great Companion.[12]

The words of another camper suggest just how completely tent life had supplanted the traditional resort hotel when he wrote how much better it was "to dwell here day after day, visiting the wonders on all hands, filling the mind with memories as enduring as itself, and returning night by night to a tent life under the shadow of eternal hills." Such a life seemed far better to "comport with the appeal of the whole panorama than a temporary home in the thronged hotel."[13]

The infatuation with tent camping affected visitors from all social and economic classes, foreign as well as domestic. While the rest of the royal party stopped at the hotel but a few miles distant, Prince Leopold of Belgium chose to camp out beside Bridalveil Creek, spending the night in a sleeping bag beneath the pines, gathering firewood, and "eating flap-jacks in such numbers as only a growing boy can encompass."[14] Camping in a tent under the stars and feasting ravenously on bacon, biscuits, and fried trout prepared over a smoking campfire were a far cry from the pretentious accommodations of an earlier era. Likewise was the manner in which tourists enjoyed their after supper hours. Rather than gather about the hotel fireplace to listen to "mine host read Scott," campers tended to gather around the campfire, singing, telling stories, and contributing impromptu readings and musical numbers. According to Foley it was not uncommon to see groups of three hundred people at a time thus engaged in enjoying the atmosphere and conviviality of the great outdoors. In prose that would have earned approbation from the most confirmed romanticist, John Burroughs reflected on his experience around a Yosemite campfire. Watching the moon come up behind Sentinel Rock, with the intermittent booming of Yosemite Falls in the background, he sensed the "tender brooding spirit of the great valley, itself touched to lyric intensity by the grandeurs on every hand, steal in upon us and possess our souls—surely that was a night none of us can ever forget."[15]

The growing popularity of camping was viewed by the Yosemite Valley commissioners with considerable apprehension. Despite the fact that they conscientiously sought to expand and improve the facilities required by campers, which included clearing additional grounds and seeding them with perennial grasses, they found much about which to complain regarding camping parties. In a report dating from the early 1890s (which could have been written last summer) the commissioners found that "campers had departed, leaving their camp grounds in an uncleanly and offensive condition, strewn with paper, cans, and trash." Equally objectionable were evidences of "painted inscriptions upon the sightly rocks and natural objects throughout the Valley." Although one of the "authors of these outrageous defacements . . . was arrested and mulcted in an exemplary fine by the local magistrate at Wawona," for the most part such vandalistic behavior represented a problem with no readily apparent solution.

Another complaint registered against campers by the commissioners was the insistence of the former, against visitor regulations, of using their road horses for travel on mountain trails. "They take the trails without guides and without regular trail animals, and without thought of the consequences fatal to themselves and others that may result from their own lack of judgement and the inexperience of their animals." Such "thoughtlessness" sometimes resulted in unfortunate accidents, two of which were described from the previous summer season. In one, a road horse ridden by a lady went over the cliff, carrying with it the rider, who, fortunately, was caught by a tree top and saved from death. In the other, a horse unaccustomed to packing, but used to carrying a camper's lunch up the same trail, went over and "was never seen nor heard of afterward."[16]

A more serious concern to the commissioners than disappearing horses was the destruction of vegetation and the perennial hazard of fire. To a man they agreed heartily with the observations of a visiting judge from Connecticut that the class of people known as "campers," that is, "people who travel with their own teams," are the source of a "great deal of damage to shrubs and smaller trees, both by cutting, by hitching their teams, and by the careless use of fire." Nevertheless, they recognized the fact, as did Judge Deming, that "this class cannot be excluded, and it would not be well to exclude them if it were possible; but the strictest rules should be made in regard to them and the most careful watch should be kept over them."[17]

In spite of the best preparations and finest of camp equipment, it could not be denied that those who chose to camp were still subjected to a certain amount of physical discomfort. To the upper-class citizens who constituted the majority of Yosemite visitors this level of accommodation was often less than acceptable. While men such as John Muir and the ever rugged Theodore Roosevelt might be impervious to personal discomforts, as one writer remarked concerning the president, "all are not as 'strenuous' as this outdoor man whom the nation honors."[18]

Despite the fact that the "rigors" and "zest" of life in the outdoors were greatly hailed as the lures which drew men to nature, tourists were reluctant to dispense with at least the minimum creature comforts to which they were accustomed. This attitude helps explain the instantaneous success of the "hotel camp" type of visitor accommodation which appeared in the Valley in the last years of the nineteenth century. According to the commissioners' report of 1897–98, the state purchased and erected a number of tents to provide accommodations for the Christian Endeavor Excursion into the Valley and thereafter began renting them to the general public on a hotel camp basis. This was not a new notion to the tourist industry; according to the commissioners this kind of thing was going on "all over the United States" before it

Figure 31. Camp Curry.

was ever introduced into the Yosemite. It had proven particularly popular in the Yellowstone, where one William H. Wiley had for several years practically dominated the business. In fact, he dominated it to the extent that later comers found it difficult to break into his market and most were forced to seek their fortunes elsewhere.

One of these unsuccessful competitors was David A. Curry who, with his wife, subsequently abandoned his Yellowstone venture and in 1899 moved to Yosemite in order to seek his fortune there. By the end of his first summer in the Valley he had entertained some three hundred persons. By 1906 the daily capacity of Camp Curry had risen to three hundred, and by 1915, one thousand. During the summer season of 1910 Camp Curry single-handedly accommodated 3,600 guests, almost a third of the entire number of Yosemite visitors for the year.[19] Curry's phenomenal success in the hotel or tent camp business prompted the creation of two other ventures of a similar nature, Camp Yosemite (later Camp Lost Arrow), located near the foot of Yosemite Falls, in 1901, and Camp Ahwahnee, at the foot of Four-Mile Trail, in 1908. Although moderately successful at first, they soon fell behind Camp Curry, which "continued for many years to stand out, head and shoulders, above all others in the way of popular appeal."[20] Camp Curry alone could and did accommodate more Yosemite visitors than either of the two hotels nearby, the Sentinel in the Valley, or the Glacier Point Mountain House on the south rim.

The immediate success of the hotel camps in attracting visitors was indicated by the fact that for the years 1908–10 more than three-fourths

Figure 32. Camp Ahwahnee.

of Yosemite's visitors chose to patronize that particular type of accommodation. This success can be attributed to several factors, one of which was the nature of the facilities themselves. Canvas tents were erected over wooden platforms and outfitted with small stoves over which, if one so desired, one could cook his/her own meals. Customarily, however, guests chose to patronize the camps' central dining rooms, in which "unostentatious but nourishing" food was served. Bathing facilities, along with improved, centrally located sanitary facilities and daily scheduled activities, provided the visitor with further conveniences which were unavailable to private camping parties. Such facilities, requiring little overhead, were also important in that they reduced greatly the cost of a Yosemite vacation, making it possible for greater numbers of people from different walks of life to visit the Yosemite. In the evenings, campfire programs rounded out the day's itinerary, providing, all things considered, a relatively inexpensive but still comfortable and socially popular way of enjoying one's Yosemite experience.

The particular success of Camp Curry can best be attributed to the fact that it provided visitors with an experience that was at once personal and highly social. In that respect Curry demonstrated that his Yellowstone venture was anything but a failure. He simply transported to Yosemite the elements that had proven popular at the Wylie Camps, whose constant aim was to "give the camps an individuality rather than to make of them a cheap substitute for hotels." Capitalizing upon the "congenial host" tradition that dated back to the days of James Hutchings, the ebullient David Curry obtained widespread popularity for his particular kind of Yosemite experience. "Big in body, mind and soul, interested in life and people, simple in his ways and habits, absolutely without any affectation, his friendly spirit and genial whole-souledness appealed to people."[21]

Curry's aim was to provide for his guests a program of complete entertainment, which included such features as a heated swimming pool, dance pavilion, and that wonder of wonders, the "firefall." Originated by James McCauley early in the 1870s, the firefall consisted of a large fire built on Glacier Point, the embers of which were pushed over the edge of the point after dark. This produced a veritable fall of fire for hundreds of feet down the face of the cliff. Although the firefall had been abandoned for years prior to Curry's arrival in the Valley, with the sure instinct of a showman he resurrected this spectacle and turned it into a nightly attraction which, over the years, achieved immense visitor popularity. Every evening Curry, who fancied himself the "Stentor" of Yosemite, boomed forth from his camp to the point above, triggering the majestic display of pyrotechnics with his awesome bellow "Let the fire fall!"

Figure 33. Mother Curry.

Figure 34. David Curry.

The ebullient personality of David Curry was augmented enormously by the "down-home" appeal of his wife, Jennie Foster Curry. Known to generations of Yosemite visitors as "Mother Curry," she injected her warm and caring personality into all aspects of the Camp Curry experience. According to one visitor Mrs. Curry was the "reigning spirit" of the camp. "She oversees everything, welcomes the guests, introducing them one to another and establishes a feeling of kindliness and good fellowship."[22]

A favorite attraction of Camp Curry was the evening camp fire. At times referred to as "faggot parties," guests often brought their own small bundles of wood to feed the flames, during which time they took their turn at telling a story, singing a song, or otherwise providing entertainment while their faggots burned. Clearly, however, the star of the daily camp fire at Camp Curry was David Curry himself. After checking to make sure that guests had taken care of their "booking for El Portal and Wawona," delivered with a sort of "rhythmical intonation peculiarly his own," he elaborated on his theories of how the Yosemite was formed. Guests responded enthusiastically to both his campfire programs and his personal charisma. At the conclusion of one such campfire program a visitor "rejoiced" that he had once again come to Camp Curry, "where the fire falls and the stentor calls."[23]

Despite whatever reservations the Yosemite Valley commissioners may have had concerning private camping in the Valley, they were both pleased with and supportive of the hotel camps. Not only did they provide a variety of visitor services but they did so in a controlled environment, minimizing both vegetation abuse and fire hazard. Furthermore, according to the commissioners, the institution of the camps resulted in considerable reduction in the cost of a trip to Yosemite, enabling many to make the trip who had heretofore been deterred from doing so by reason of the expense. The cost of living at the camps was less than two dollars per day, which was probably as low a rate as could reasonably be expected, considering the distance of the Valley from railroad terminals and the consequent expense of getting supplies into the Valley.[24]

Just as camping had become the fashionable way to spend a night in the Yosemite, so had hiking become the chief means of visiting its scenic attractions. Only by tramping through the forests and up the mountain trails on foot, maintained outdoors enthusiasts of the Muir cast, could one really become "in tune" with the beauties and essence of nature. By the end of the nineteenth century Yosemite guidebooks were encouraging tourists to first take to the trails and then, if they so desired, to take advantage of the Valley's "other" attractions. And yet prior to the 1890s there were few trails that were considered acceptable for strictly pedestrian use. As late as 1886 the commissioners reported that there was not a footpath in the Valley. In their attempts to obtain more money for long-needed improvements they bemoaned the fact that there were no "practicable footways for ladies to the foot of Yosemite Falls and Illilouette Falls." Those who did care to "tramp" about the Valley or ascend into the High Sierra beyond were forced to

Figure 35. Sally Dutcher, first woman on Half Dome.

compete with horses on the regular trails, where they existed, or to pick their own way or follow game and sheep trails, which seldom led the hiker to an intended destination.

In 1890 the Yosemite High Sierra achieved national park status and the United States Army was brought in to administer it. Under army supervision a network of trails was constructed that more or less persists to this day. In 1906 the original Yosemite grant, which included the Valley and its immediate environs, as well as the Mariposa Grove of Giant Sequoia, was receded to the United States government and added to the existing national park. Military engineers subsequently continued their trail-building efforts throughout the Valley and around the surrounding rim. Prior to this time most of Yosemite's trails had been built almost exclusively for saddle and pack animals, with apparently little consideration given to use by hikers. During the national park conference of 1912 the acting military superintendent of the Yosemite National Park, aware of the increasingly heavy use of the trails by hikers, recommended that the entire trail system in the park be improved to more adequately meet the needs of pedestrians.

Another advocate of an improved trail system urged the introduction of specifically "pedestrian tours" as opposed to pack-in camping trips. Acknowledging that hiking and camping were often the only means whereby "the fastnesses of our mountains may be reached and explored," he nevertheless pointed out that "its pleasures and profits were often purchased at the cost of so much labor, anxiety, and positive

Figure 36. Evening around the campfire, 1899.

discomfort" as to raise the question, was there no alternative? Elsewhere, he claimed, in the White Mountains and the Adirondacks, in England, Scotland, and Switzerland, the pedestrian tour was "deservedly popular, and largely takes the place of our western camping-trip." Two conditions were needed to achieve that success, however, and in his opinion the Sierra Nevada Mountains were seriously deficient in both: "well-marked routes and the assurance of reaching each night some good, comfortable harborages." Were these deficiencies to be remedied, he maintained, there would result a tremendous increase in the number of people who would be inclined to include a trip to California in their outdoor vacation plans. While he readily conceded that such "improvements" might be looked upon with disdain by the more hardy of the Sierra hikers, he pointed out that many others there doubtless were who were less "supremely endowed with strength and ambition," persons who could enjoy an "exhilarating walk or climb," even if there was no great hardship or danger involved. These were people who could, "without utter loss of self-respect," look forward to a good dinner and bed at the end of each day's tramp, who could feel the "charm and inspiration of noble scenery" no less because it was not quite inaccessible to all others.[25]

Despite these apparent obstacles Yosemite visitors "took to the trails" in ever increasing numbers. Such trends were a great satisfaction to John Muir, who rejoiced that so many young men and women growing up in California were going to the mountains every summer and becoming "good mountaineers, and, of course, good defenders of the Sierra forests and of all the reviving beauty that belongs to them." For every one that he had found mountaineering in the Yosemite High Sierra ten years earlier, in the middle 1890s he reported meeting more than a hundred. Many of these young mountaineers were girls, in parties of ten or fifteen, making "bright pictures as they tramped merrily along through the forest aisles, with the sparkle and exhilaration of the mountains in their eyes—a fine, hopeful sign of the times."[26]

Along with camping and hiking, other forms of outdoor recreation were popular in this period. By the turn of the century the national parks were increasingly referred to as America's "playgrounds," in which a variety of outdoor activities were appropriate. In the Yosemite, according to one guidebook author, "Snow sports in winter, dancing, campfire festivities, fishing and climbing in the summer are the Valley's amusements."[27] Especially popular was the Camp Curry swimming pool. After a rigorous day of tramping about the Valley the luxury and relaxation of Curry's heated pool were (shades of Hutchings' ghost!) "not to be despised." For those who were young enough to desire more action than the evening campfire programs provided, "one of the most popular places during the summer season" was the government dance pavilion, "well lighted by electricity," where "dancing socials (were) held twice a week during the summer and fall months."[28]

On June 4, 1892 a group of San Franciscans, including several Stanford University and University of California, Berkeley professors, met to organize the Sierra Club, an organization dedicated to "exploring, enjoying and rendering accessible the mountain regions of the Pacific Coast." For its first president the club elected John Muir, who remained in that office until his death twenty-two years later. Although not the first of its kind on the Pacific coast, the Sierra Club was destined to become not only the largest in the West but also by far the most influential. From its beginning the club assumed the mantle of citizen/guardian of the Yosemite, dedicated to protecting and utilizing its resources according to the club's own particular definitions of national park philosophy. The club's founders were motivated, like their counterparts elsewhere, by an enthusiasm for the outdoor life and a desire to see it promulgated as widely as possible. They also felt a keen sense of responsibility for the mountains and a sincere desire to engage themselves in efforts to protect their scenic resources. In this sense they reflected both the progressive spirit of their times and the traditions of other mountaineering clubs such as Oregon's Mazamas, whose object, like that of similar societies in Europe, was to stimulate in people a "love of the mountains, and to awaken an interest in the study of them, and yearly to accomplish something which, besides reflecting credit upon the members, should benefit the world."[29]

As suggested by Kevin Starr, the Sierra Club represented a flowering of ecological stewardship on the part of California's upper middle classes. Of the one hundred sixty-two charter members of the club, most were university educated professional men, together with a large representation from the faculties at Palo Alto and Berkeley. The traditional elite of society and the very wealthy were noticeably absent from the club's charter ranks. Members of the Sierra Club, like the vast majority of outdoors enthusiasts, represented a major break from earlier tourist society wherein wealth, social status, and fashion were considered paramount in determining one's ability to understand and appreciate nature. As personified by John Muir, the new generation of nature lovers boldly maintained that a sensitive and willing spirit and a responsive intellect were the principal qualifiers that enabled one to best comprehend and enjoy the beauties of nature.

There existed in the Sierra Club and its counterparts a sense of belonging and elitism every bit as strong as that felt in the "Newport" crowd, although based upon different criteria. Membership in Newport's glittering summer society was largely by birthright, although such a birthright could be purchased if the aspiring member was wealthy enough. Membership in the fraternity of the outdoors, however, was, in the best American tradition, something that had to be earned. Illustrating the kind of qualifications that were popularly considered necessary for one to become a genuine "mountaineer" is this statement of Robert Sterling Yard, a national parks advocate and prominent easterner. Appearing before the National Park Conference of 1915, he apologized for the vocation and place of residence that had prevented him from becoming a true outdoorsman.

> Mr. Secretary and friends, I have no business to be here, as I think you all know, for the reason that I am a tenderfoot. I have no right to stand up here talking to mountaineers. Nevertheless I have got the stuff inside of me. When I am in the woods I feel closer to God than anywhere else. I think the hour of the deepest devotion and the highest spiritual uplift of all my life was an hour I spent all alone, solitary and silent, in a great beech woods in the northeastern corner of the Adirondacks. I have not qualified for the Rocky Mountains. But I know I shall qualify, because the qualification for the mountains, as I well know, lies inside of one, lies in the soul, and not in one's accomplishments. So it is that I, the treader of dusty city streets, boldly claim common kinship with you of the plains, the mountains, and the glaciers. For the love that is in your hearts is also in mine. There is the human appeal that is our common possession.[30]

Perhaps the best way to understand the operations, the popularity, and the "magic" of the early Sierra Club is through that most popular of club institutions, the annual outing. Begun in 1901, the outings incorporated a happy combination of fun, fellowship, and edification that would characterize the outings for years to follow. It should be pointed out that the above ingredients were neither original nor unique to the Sierra Club. Similar programs had been in existence at Atlantic coast seaside resorts for more than half a century. The chautauqua organization had also successfully demonstrated a mixture of outdoor recreation activities, social comradery, and intellectual edification that was popular nation-wide. Nevertheless, the annual outing of the Sierra Club rapidly took on a flavor that was to achieve for the club both immense local popularity and a national reputation. Most importantly, perhaps, in the context of the Yosemite, it was the outings that influenced so many of Yosemite's visitors to become imbued with the attitudes and philosophies of nature that best represented the great outdoors era.

The first of the Sierra Club's annual outings took place in the Yosemite High Sierra, in Tuolumne Meadows, during the summer of 1901. Over one hundred persons were included, along with supply wagons, mule trains, and full-time chefs. From their base camps parties or individuals, if they so desired, struck out on their own to various parts of the High Sierra, returning at night to the fellowship and hot food of the main camp. Much of the spirit and purpose of that first outing can be gleaned from the report of William E. Colby, head of the committee that had been organized to plan the outing. Colby's comments indicate clearly that the key ingredients that were to characterize and do so much to popularize the outings were carefully premeditated, and, incidentally, not particularly original to the Sierra Club. "The Mazamas and Appalachian Clubs have for many years shown how successful and interesting such trips may be made." Along with John Muir, various faculty members from Stanford and Berkeley were invited to provide campfire lectures on the natural sciences. And to insure "the high class and tone" of the trip, "only members of the club and their immediate friends (were) eligible to join the party."[31]

From all indications the 1901 outing was a complete success. What had apparently been a concern to some, that being with such a large party would be unpleasant to lovers of nature more "accustomed" to solitude, "proved entirely without foundation." Rather, reported a participant from that trip, "the association with so many genial spirits, and the valuable instruction obtained from the learned lights of the party, made it a pleasure and a memory never to be forgotten."[32] Comments from participants on the first as well as on subsequent outings emphasized the fact that such "association" was one of the principal satisfactions of the trips. A midwestern school teacher who had been apprehensive about the sociability of the group was extremely gratified to find that the party was made up of "sociable people who fell naturally into the unconventialities of camp life," and who met one with that "frank and hearty manner that makes getting acquainted easy, and that causes one to feel that one's friendship is considered a favor."[33]

The very nature of camp life and such physically vigorous activities as hiking and swimming tended to break down social barriers and foster

Figure 37. The dance pavilion.

a general spirit of comradery. Such "comradery," to the happy surprise of some, encompassed members of both sexes. Nearly all of the women in his party, observed one participant, were Berkeley or Stanford girls, whose vigor and endurance were a "revelation to all of us, demonstrating as they did that health and vigor go with college life." At no time during the outing did the college women give out or find fault, he went on to note, nor did they delay or "prove a drag on the progress of the excursion." One confirmed mountaineer said that it was the first time he had ever been camping with women, and that he had started in with "serious misgivings, but after this experience he would never go to the mountains again without the added pleasure of the companionship of women." Whether he did or did not follow through on this resolve, it is a fact that he and a fellow outing participant were subsequently married. It is also a fact that they were among the most enthusiastic participants of the annual outings for years to come—E. T. and Marion Randall Parsons.[34]

As was the case at Camp Curry, the evenings spent around the campfires were among the most popular elements of an outing experience. It was on these occasions that the happy combination of fun, fellowship, and edification that gave social substance to the outings was crystallized. For many participants the outings represented a definition of congenial democracy that was a new experience. And nowhere was this better expressed than around the evening campfire, where "grave professors, giddy co-eds, the poet, the historian, and sundry medical, clerical, and legal lights blushed alike in the camp-fire's rosy glow."[35] All were expected to contribute something for the edification and/or entertainment of the others. Songs—sometimes accompanied by in-

Figure 38. Campfire in Tuolumne Meadows, 1927.

struments packed in expressly for that purpose—were followed by stories, recitations, and even practical jokes on fellow members of the party. In a more serious vein the warmth and informality of the campfires prompted newly-made friends to share with each other their "most cherished ideas and dearest ambitions, aspirations, and confidences."[36] It was no wonder that, especially in a social context, the evenings around the campfire meant so much to outing participants.

> These camp-fire gatherings hold a place among your dearest recollections of the summer. The faces that you have seen illumined by the leaping flames can never be indifferent to you, and wheresoever you may meet them, in crowded streets or dingy offices, or in the heat and babble of an afternoon tea, they will bring to you a little thrill of joy as if you caught again a breath from the pines.[37]

Without doubt the Sierra Club outings became one of the most popular institutions of their time. Socially, emotionally, and philosophically, the outings synthesized the essence of what was most characteristic of the great outdoors era: "comradeship and chivalry, simplicity and joyousness, and the care-free life of the open."

Despite the great popularity of the Sierra Club, not all Yosemite visitors shared club members' enthusiasm for life in the rough. Traditional romanticists, hotel-bound and elitist though they were, still constituted a significant minority whose influence usually far exceeded their numbers. Throughout the period there was a constant stream of recommendations regarding the need for a first class hotel in the Valley as well as additional facilities located nearer key attractions. One guidebook author recommended that a hotel be built on top of Half Dome, reached by an elevator that would be supplied with electricity generated by a turbine built at Nevada Fall. From time to time there were movements to construct roads leading up out of the Valley beyond both Tenaya Lake and the Nevada Fall region. To the traditionalist mind, it should be remembered, such roads not only could serve as means of comfortable access to scenic points but also could be considered to have esthetic appeal in and of themselves. T. Warren Allen, of the United States Department of Agriculture's Office of Public Roads, dreamed of seeing such roads "lined and banked with the flowers which grow wild in the meadows of the parks and upon the mountain sides, winding unassumingly along the brook, beneath the waterfall, and skirting timidly the majestic mountain."[38]

More roads and better hotels were not the only "improvements" recommended by more traditional visitors. In keeping with the resort mentality that had characterized romanticists of an earlier generation, a variety of developments was advocated in an attempt to attract more of the "right" kind of tourists to the Yosemite. At the National Park Conference of 1911 U. S. Geological Survey official Robert B. Marshall lamented the lack of such developments when he pointed out that in Yosemite there were no attractions save an "unkept nature's wonderland." There were any number of people, he maintained, who would travel miles for the pleasure of golf, tennis, open-air concerts, skating, skiing, sleighing, and similar attractions. "Such civilized attractions would add much to the physical pleasure to thousands of the people of California alone, to say nothing of the people from other States, or even the world." Marshall went further to suggest that even the secretary of the Interior would be tempted to "forget the affairs of state and make at least one trip a year to the Yosemite for a chance to put a ball over the bunker, El Capitan, with a Mono Indian for a caddy."[39]

It should come as no surprise to find that Mr. Marshall also advocated selective timber harvesting and cattle grazing on national park lands, maintaining that the latter "would keep the trails open and (control) the underbrush." What is more surprising, perhaps, is the response to Marshall's recommendations of Horace McFarland, well-known friend and advocate of the national parks, who saw no objection to what Marshall had said as to using the mature timber and permitting the grazing. They were matters of administration which needed to be worked out, he felt. "Any legitimate and proper usage of the advantages and resources of the parks and monuments is bound to be beneficial."[40]

While such compromise was abhorrent to John Muir, it is important to realize that Muir did not represent all lovers of the national parks or even of Yosemite. The preservation of park landscapes as undeveloped wilderness was not an important ingredient of the great outdoors philosophy of nature. Rather, most visitors to and friends of the national parks would have agreed with Major William Forsyth, acting superintendent of Yosemite National Park, that "the object for which these parks were set aside . . . was (for) the benefit and enjoyment of the people whether or not the law setting them aside specifically so stated."[41] In providing for the "benefit and enjoyment of the people" it was not deemed necessary to exclude from the parks developments whose principal design was to enhance visitor satisfaction in a traditional resort sense. In this context we can better understand a man like Robert Marshall, who did not see as inconsistent the utilization of national park resources by timber and cattle operations. To the contrary, Marshall perceived himself as a loyal defender and enthusiastic proponent of the parks.

> I want each of you to know and to love our national playgrounds as I do, to feel their inspiration, to have worlds of friends in the old storm-seared peaks, the trees, the birds, the flowers, the streams, the animals, all beckoning, calling to you to come and live among them. And when you can rush away from the busy life and go to them they will greet you smiling and laughing, swaying all about in genuine glee as do children greeting their favorite playmates. Oh, it is glorious beyond description, and so satisfying. The wonders of the parks can never be told; you must go to them and absorb their influences.[42]

In a day when to many the very size of the national parks appeared to be more than adequate protection against "inappropriate" exploitation, the philosophical "inconsistencies" of men like Marshall did not seem particularly significant. These attitudes do help to explain, however, the willingness with which Californians acceded to the proposals of the city of San Francisco to construct a dam in Yosemite's Hetch Hetchy Valley for the purpose of providing the city with a municipal water supply. The Hetch Hetchy affair also was a pointed reminder that the influence of John Muir and the Sierra Club was not dominant in California, or even in Yosemite. For despite the energetic campaign waged by the club to save Hetch Hetchy from development, in the end it was the Californians themselves who chose to build the dam.

With the opening of the Yosemite Valley Railroad in 1907 the cost of visiting the Valley from San Francisco via public transportation was reduced by two-thirds, from about $75.00 to $22.35. Although that did much to alleviate the burdensome costs of a visit to the Yosemite it should not be inferred that such a trip was affordable by the general population. An interesting and revealing comment to this effect was made by E. T. Parsons at the national parks conference of 1912. "I have been waiting since the beginning of this meeting for a certain class and their opportunities and rights to be mentioned," he said. "We are discussing at great length the automobilists. We have been discussing the ordinary traveler, who has the money to come and go; but nobody has said a word for the shopgirl, working for $8 or $10 or $12 a week, and the clerk who may get $12 or $15 a week, and has a beggarly week or ten days or less." In Parsons' opinion, and his comments suggested that the actual situation was otherwise, "these parks ought to be open to them."[43]

While it was true that a Yosemite vacation was not yet within the reach of the common American, it was also true that during the great outdoors era the spectrum of visitors able to afford a Yosemite experience had broadened considerably. Camping and hiking, in becoming the most popular way "to do" the Yosemite, had also done much to democratize the Yosemite experience by reducing many of the costs appertaining thereto. In the meantime, there awaited at the gates of the Valley a noisy, mechanically undependable, and generally unlovely contrivance that was destined to bring a vacation trip to the Yosemite within the financial reach of almost every stratum of American society. The automobile, the "infernal machine," would finally be allowed legal entry into the Valley in 1913, and the Yosemite would never again be the same.

Chapter 5

The Nation's Playgrounds

ON AUGUST 25, 1916 President Woodrow Wilson signed into law legislation creating the National Park Service. Friends and supporters of the national parks were ecstatic. For over forty years, since the establishment of Yellowstone as the country's first official "national park" in 1872, the administration and care of the parks had been a rather ill-defined and admittedly secondary concern of the Department of the Interior. With the creation of an official agency designed specifically to deal with them, it was felt that the national parks at last had come of age. In the minds of park supporters the creation of the National Park Service promised solution to several of the parks' most vexing problems. Up to that point, as evidenced by the tragic loss of Hetch Hetchy, national park landscapes were still considered by many Americans as "open opportunity" lands whose value to the nation lay not so much in their preservation as scenic or unique environments but rather in their grazing, mineral, and timber potential. The National Parks Act promised a degree of protection from these exploitative interests hitherto unknown in the history of the parks.

Of equal importance to park advocates was the hope that with the creation of the Park Service would come a systematic development program aimed at making the parks more accessible to the traveling public. Some of the most enthusiastic support for such development came from members of a new group of pleasure travelers, those who chose to travel in that "new-fangled" contraption, the automobile. At first the toy of the rich man, the automobile, with its distinct advantages of mobility and versatility, was soon established as a means of transportation endowed with almost limitless possibilities. As expressed by a contemporary "automobilist," "in a little more than twenty years the automobile has revolutionized the average American's vacation, it has brought about a renaissance of the outdoors, and it has firmly planted a brand-new out-door sport."[1]

Figure 39. Yosemite via Stanley Steamer, 1900.

Autocamping, as the new sport was called, introduced all sorts of new and exciting "wrinkles" to camping. Principal among these were greater mobility and increased baggage-carrying capacity, both of which added considerably to the range and comfort of the individual camper. Prior to that time the railroads were the chief means of conveyance for pleasure travelers, and although trains provided comfort and speed on a scale never before imagined, they nevertheless imposed certain limitations on their customers. With the advent of the automobile, travelers not only could range considerably farther afield but also could free themselves, if they wished, from the more constraining environment and higher costs of the resort hotels. Autocampers, an increasing percentage of whom perceived camping as a means of stretching their vacation dollar, were particularly cognizant of this latter advantage. They also appreciated the considerable baggage capacity of the automobile. Perhaps in an over-reaction to "traveling light" via the railroads, autocampers enthusiastically equipped their vehicles quite literally as homes on wheels. Given the condition of contemporary roads and accommodations facilities, such preparation was probably as practical as it was fashionable.

The rapidly growing popularity of autocamping resulted in an accompanying surge in national parks visitation. Quick to recognize this trend was Stephen T. Mather, the first director of the Park Service, who maintained that the perfection of the automobile as a reliable and comfortable means of transportation had undoubtedly had most to do with stimulating travel to the national parks.[2] A dynamic and successful

Figure 40. Automobile campers, 1927

salesman, Mather was also an automobilist and outdoorsman. From the beginning he repeatedly and enthusiastically encouraged the nation's growing number of automobile owners to visit the national parks. One of his first acts as director of the Park Service was to abolish the various restrictions that prohibited the entry and/or use of automobiles in the parks. He strongly supported such ventures as the National Park-to-Park Highway Association, a group of automobilists interested in the creation of a paved, six thousand-mile loop road which would connect twelve of the western national parks in one grand circuit. Across the nation he cooperated with automobile clubs and chambers of commerce in promoting automobile travel and the construction and expansion of municipal and private autocamping facilities. Within the parks themselves he pushed for improved roads and accommodations designed especially for use by automobilists.

A man of democratic vision, Mather foresaw a time when the national parks would be accessible to every American family. He viewed the automobile, with its versatility and relative economy, as an important means of facilitating this goal. To a certain extent, it was already happening. For the first time the national parks were coming within the reach of the middle classes. Prior to this time, in spite of the ameliorating effects of the railroads, national park travel had been quite effectively restricted to the affluent. And although a trip to one or more of the national parks was still an expensive luxury for the average American and virtually impossible for those of less than average income, the spectrum of national park visitors was wider than it had ever been before. "The automobile and the municipal camps have so cheapened travel," recognized a writer in Sunset, "that the wonders of the West's national parks today are accessible to hundreds of thousands who ten years ago had as much chance to see them as Hobson has of becoming admiral of the Swiss navy."[3]

The effect of the automobile was felt immediately in the Yosemite. In 1915, after little more than one year of legal automobile access, more than twice as many visitors came to the park than before automobiles had been allowed entry. The figure continued to double itself every several years thereafter until finally slowed by the Great Depression. Of equal importance was the rapid increase of the automobile as the chief means of conveyance. By 1922 over 65 percent of Yosemite's visitors were coming by private automobile, a figure greater by six times than the largest number of people ever to visit the park in one season prior to 1915. During this same season, 1922, 24 percent came via the Yosemite Valley Railroad, representing in itself almost a 100 percent absolute increase over the total number of pre-1915 visitors per season. One decade later, however, there were almost eight times as many automobiles in the park, which accounted for 97 percent of all visitors for the year. Conversely, railroad travel dropped both absolutely and relatively. Furthermore, those visitors who continued to patronize the railroad in their Yosemite tours tended to be wealthy non-Californians, mostly easterners. What this essentially meant to Yosemite tourist patterns was that in addition to the enormous rate of annual visitor increase Yosemite tourists were mainly automobilists and hailed from some part of California. It was estimated in 1929 that more than 85 percent of Yosemite's visitors were residents of the Golden State.[4]

Yosemite Valley continued to be the principal objective of the park's burgeoning numbers of tourists. In spite of the fact that prior to 1926 most tourists entered the Yosemite on the Wawona Road, only half as many visited the Wawona and Mariposa Big Tree Grove region as visited the Valley. With the completion of the shorter, all-weather road up the Merced River Canyon, the Wawona-Mariposa Grove section of the park declined significantly in relative importance. And even though the Tioga Road, on which visitors entered the park from the east over the High Sierra, became increasingly popular, by far the greatest number of tourists visiting the Yosemite utilized the new road up the Merced Canyon through El Portal into the Valley. It was opened the first of August, 1926, and during the following month the previous August's travel count more than doubled. Although trains continued to run twice daily they never again functioned as a primary means of transit into the Yosemite.

The explosive growth in national park visitation that characterized the 1920s was a source of great satisfaction to Director Mather. In such growth, he felt, lay the ultimate security of the parks. Among the problems facing the National Park Service at its creation, two of the most pressing had been the protection of park landscapes from traditional, "exploitative" enemies and the development of the parks in such a way that the public could enjoy what they had to offer. The ultimate solution to both of these problems, as envisioned by Mather, was a swelling, grass-roots popularity of the national parks among the American people. Only as the public came to understand and appreciate the parks, he felt, would they rise to protect and cherish them. In this respect he spent himself lavishly spreading national park publicity and making "friends for the parks." In his efforts to popularize them Mather forged a two-pronged attack. His first goal was to get more people into the national parks, and the second, after they had come, was to keep them there for longer periods of time. Clearly these goals were inseparable; he could not expect to draw large crowds of tourists without something inside the parks to attract and hold them. On the other hand, large-scale developments within the parks could not realistically be made without sufficient numbers of tourists to support them.

Mather's response to these challenges took the form of a vigorous campaign carried forward along three broad fronts: first, to keep up with growing numbers of visitors it was imperative that visitor accommodations of a wide variety of types be expanded and upgraded—people needed to find in the parks the level of services to which they were accustomed; second, virtually all kinds of recreation attractions normally associated with a vacation experience were to be encouraged within the national park setting, with emphasis upon those activities traditionally associated with the great outdoors; and third, there needed to be developed within the parks programs that would both enrich and educate visitors as to the value of the national parks in America. It was to the successful accomplishment of these objectives that Mather committed the strength of the National Park Service and the remaining fifteen years of his life.

The rapid growth of national park visitation that characterized the 1920s was as much a challenge as it was a blessing. In none of the parks were roads and visitor facilities adequate to deal with such an increase.

Particularly was this true regarding overnight visitor accommodations. In their attempts to provide satisfactory accommodations Park Service officials followed guidelines set down by Mark Daniels at the National Park Conference of 1915, scarcely a year preceding the creation of the National Park Service. At that time Daniels was acting as general superintendent and landscape engineer of the national parks. At this conference he proposed the establishment of three classifications of accommodations in the parks: first, the hotel or the mountain chalet; second, the permanent camp, where tourists slept in tents and took their meals in a dining room; and third, the camp where tourists both ate and slept in a rented tent. He later recognized the need for a fourth class of accommodations, designed to fill the needs of those who chose to bring with them their complete camp outfit.[5] With the exception of the first of these, Yosemite was rather well-equipped to handle and expand these various kinds of facilities. At times, upwards of a dozen public campgrounds dotted the upper Valley floor, while the Yosemite Lodge, which utilized the remaining military occupation structures, and Camp Curry managed to expand at a pace sufficient to meet most of the needs of the tent and permanent camp category of visitors.

The most serious deficiency in Yosemite accommodations, according to Mather and a number of other similarly-inclined travelers, was the absence of a truly first-class hotel in the Yosemite Valley. The old Sentinel Hotel was generally acknowledged as inadequate, while the newer Glacier Point Hotel, built in 1917, was neither centrally located

Figure 41. Stephen T. Mather, center, first director of the National Park Service, with California Governor Richardson, left, and Harvey Toy, California Highway Commission chairman.

nor elegant enough to meet the demands of Yosemite's luxury-seeking classes. And while Mather and his associates might have been egalitarian in philosophy they tended to be more patrician in their personal preferences. Besides, Mather justifiably maintained that America's national parks could never hope to compete as world-class vacation destinations until the level of their visitor services improved accordingly. As Mark Daniels pointed out, world travelers of the type most desirable in the parks were not likely to respond to even the greatest of natural wonders if they were forced to put up with "a cot under a pine tree and a diet of bacon and beans." "From a record of travel in our parks, it may be shown that the finest scenery without accommodations will not receive so large a travel as an inferior character of scenery which has a better type of accommodations."[6] Confirming his sentiments almost a decade later, Mather wrote in 1923 that "the finest scenery, without adequate accommodations, is never as popular or receives so large a travel as scenery of lesser quality with good accommodations."[7] More directly to the point, "scenery is a hollow enjoyment to a tourist who sets out in the morning after an indigestible breakfast and a fitful sleep on an impossible bed."[8]

The construction during 1926 of the luxurious Ahwahnee Hotel promised to satisfy, at last, the demand for a truly first-class accommodation in the Yosemite. First opened for business in 1927, it was an expensive, elaborately furnished and landscaped stone structure whose "rugged massive walls reflected the ageless granite cliffs which sur-

Figure 42. Autos awaiting entrance to Yosemite Valley.

Figure 43. The Ahwahnee Hotel.

rounded the Valley," and whose interior, "decorated with the beauty and simplicity of Indian design, reflected the spirit of the early Indian inhabitants of Yosemite, who called their home 'Ahwahnee,' meaning 'Deep Grassy Valley.'"[9]

Mather's efforts to expand visitor accommodation facilities in Yosemite were not limited to the Valley. In his 1923 annual report to the secretary of the Interior he wrote glowingly of Yosemite's High Sierra back country, "considerable of which has heretofore been little seen because of lack of proper facilities." Despite the fact that the High Sierra was "an ideal country for the hiker or foot traveler," many visitors were unable to enjoy it due to "the necessity of having . . . to pack (in) all food supplies, bedding, etc. in order to penetrate it." To remedy these difficulties, a scheme was developed for the establishment of semi-permanent camps at Merced Lake, Tuolumne Meadows, and Tenaya Lake, where the simplest and least expensive accommodations possible could be offered those who chose to tramp the High Sierra on foot. Each camp was to consist of three large tents, capable of accommodating sixteen or eighteen people, and were to be used as cooking and dining facilities and sleeping quarters for men and women. The sleeping accommodations were to consist only of folding cots and blankets and the meals of the simplest cooked foods, "principally canned stuff, but all wholesome." The advantages of these camps, in Mather's mind, were several: not only were expenses of transportation reduced but also "the necessity of burdening one's self with supplies and bedding" were largely obviated. Most importantly, these camps were to offer "reasonably comfortable accommodations and wholesome meals (offering) the real lover of the mountains an opportunity to see the back country at a minimum of expense."[10] As a statement of official policy the foregoing was of deep importance. To Mather and his associates the pleasure to be derived from nature was not necessarily related to the rigors of backpacking; rather, the fullest enjoyment of the great outdoors could be obtained only when one was not unduly "burdened" with the mundane necessities required for life therein. This relationship between creature comforts and enjoyment of nature persisted throughout the Mather era and, following his untimely death near the close of the 1920s, was perpetuated for several decades by his associates, who formed the framework of "the house that Mather built."

Mather's schemes for national park development did not end with accommodations. Improved roads and better access to scenic points were also promoted energetically by him and his colleagues in the Service. In Yosemite this included plans for a tramway which would run from the Valley to Glacier Point, as some means of rapid transportation between the two was felt to be necessary for "the best enjoyment of the park by the public."[11] Another of his development schemes which never materialized was his plan to construct an access road eastward out of the Valley into the High Sierra. The road was to follow the Merced River up past Vernal and Nevada Falls into the Little Yosemite Valley, thence connecting with the Tioga Road at Tenaya Lake. According to Mather, the survey was "carefully run so as not to interfere with the beauty of the falls."[12]

The first of Mather's objectives designed to promote greater visitation to the national parks was the development of all manner of visitor

Figure 44. High Sierra hikers, Merced Lake camp.

services. The second was the provision of an array of attractions that would both satisfy visitors and encourage them to plan for a longer stay in the parks. In this sense he was an enthusiastic adherent to the growing notion that the national parks' destiny was to be the "playgrounds of the nation." Throughout the entire system of parks he enthusiastically encouraged such outdoor sports as hiking, camping, riding, swimming, fishing, and, later, all forms of winter sports. He simultaneously endorsed such "artificial" amusements as dancing, bowling, and billiards. His concept of national park use involved development of practically all forms of recreation and sport, with the ever-present goal in mind of continually increasing the attractiveness of the parks to the vacationing public. "Golf links, tennis courts, swimming pools, and other equipment for outdoor pastime and exercise should be provided by concessions," he maintained, "and the park should be extensively advertised as a place to spend the summer instead of five or six days of hurried sightseeing under constant pressure to keep moving."[13]

One aspect of outdoor recreation that Mather hoped would become "a great feature" in the parks was winter sports. Snow sports in the Yosemite had been popular at least as early as 1914, when such activities as snowshoeing, ice skating, and sliding on ash can lids drew "many parties to the Valley each winter."[14] By the early 1920s three to four thousand persons were visiting the Valley during the winter

Figure 45. Horseback riders in Yosemite Valley, 1938.

months, and Mather was enthusiastically predicting that with the construction of a new, modern hotel and "an easy means of access to Glacier Point" Yosemite would rank "among the greatest winter resorts of the world."[15]

Always anxious to improve business conditions, the Yosemite Park and Curry Company established the Yosemite Winter Club in 1928 and during the course of the winter of 1929–30 opened their new ski-touring lodge at Snow Creek. Foreign ski instructors were hired and a host of winter sports activities were sponsored by the company. In his annual report of 1930, Mather's successor as director of the Park Service, Horace Albright, praised the Yosemite Park & Curry Company for "contributing heavily to Yosemite's year-round usefulness by emphasizing the development of winter sports." High points of the winter's activities included the sponsorship of a championship cup by President Hoover, won by the University of California. Speed-skating and figure-skating experts gave special exhibitions and numerous "appropriate" contests were organized. Over 100,000 visitors participated variously in tobogganing, skating, sleighing, snowshoeing, etc. Two teams of "husky" dogs contributed "atmosphere and keen enjoyment." The ski lodge at Snow Creek was maintained by the company for snow sports available in that vicinity and as a snow-shoe rest house on the winter route to the Tuolumne region. Expert instructors were available throughout the season, which closed February 22. Albright concluded

Figure 46. Snowshoers at Glacier Point Hotel.

Figure 47. The Ice Rink in Yosemite Valley, 1933.

Figure 48. Yosemite winter sports enthusiasts.

Figure 49. Badger Pass ski house.

by stating that despite generally unfavorable weather the company's winter program "was a wholesome and picturesque public service."[16] Snow conditions improved during the next few winters and ski lodges were opened at Tenaya Lake and Tuolumne Meadows. These ski-touring facilities for cross country skiing were relatively unimportant in terms of numbers accommodated, however; the Valley was the scene for by far the greatest amount of winter activity. Popular activities ranged from skijoring, dog sledding, and sleigh rides to evening skating competitions, costume carnivals, and curling.[17] (Skijoring involved an adventurous skier being towed along the snow by a horse, presumably one trained to avoid logs, rocks, and other hazards.)

Snow sports reached their full development in Yosemite during the 1930s with the construction at Badger Pass of a new ski lodge and alpine or downhill run facilities. Prior to this time skiing had been participated in mainly on the small slopes within the Valley or in the High Sierra in the form of ski-touring, or cross country skiing. With the completion of the Badger Pass facilities in 1935 Yosemite assumed the function of a well-equipped and popular winter resort, complete with luxurious accommodations, equipment shops, and ski lifts leading to a series of well-defined downhill ski runs. Badger Pass became the most popular of Yosemite's winter sports areas, and as more enthusiasts became enamored with its location and facilities, winter sports in other areas of the park declined in importance. Although activities persisted in the Valley the ski huts scattered about the High Sierra were eventually abandoned.

The third thrust of Mather's campaign to "sell" the parks to the traveling public was the development of programs designed to educate visitors regarding the true value of national parks in America. According to Mather this concept of park use represented the highest stage of an ongoing evolution of national park perceptions. Initial notions of national parks as "stupendous natural spectacles" were followed by the perception of parks as outdoor vacation centers. "Lastly is the realization," he wrote, "that our parks are not only show places and vacation lands but also vast school-rooms of Americanism where people are studying, enjoying, and learning to love more deeply this land in which they live."[18] Perhaps the most cherished of Mather's dreams for the national parks was that they become "school-rooms of Americanism," permanent outdoor exhibits reflecting the very best elements and ideals of the American way of life.

In Yosemite and, for that matter, the national park system as a whole, the nature interpretation program was initiated formally during the summer of 1920 when doctors Harold C. Bryant and Loye H. Miller began conducting campfire talks and nature study walks in the Valley. For several seasons prior to this Bryant had conducted similar activities at Lake Tahoe, and it was there that Mather saw the possibilities of such work in the national parks. In his own inimitable way Mather convinced Bryant to transfer his activities to Yosemite where the "nature guide service" soon became one of the most popular attractions in the park. During the 1920s nature lore spread like a fever; "everyone" felt it. "Visitors to the parks were formerly satisfied to admire scenic features," rejoiced Mather; "now they want to understand them. The spirit of wanting to know is felt everywhere."[19]

It was Mather's dream that the national parks take a leading role in proclaiming nature as "the supreme schoolteacher as well as the master textbook." Every aspect of the evolving nature interpretation program operated on the basic philosophy that "from Nature can be learned the scheme of creation and the handiwork of the Great Architect as from no other source."[20] Under the joint planning of Mather and his assistants the Yosemite nature guide service took shape along the following lines: first, field trips conducted by nature guides competent to explain every subject of natural history observed along the trailside; second, camp fire lectures on birds, geology, or any of the other phases of nature "so wonderfully exemplified" in the parks; third, collection of materials that could best be presented in a simple, systematic way in order to tell the story of the parks. These collections formed the nuclei for the museums; and fourth, field courses in various branches of natural history offered by the Park Service in cooperation with universities and other institutions.[21]

Field trips and campfire lectures were the first of these objectives to be successfully implemented in the park. Following closely, Yosemite museum collections began to take shape under the personal initiative of Ranger Ansel F. Hall. By 1926 a new museum building had been constructed and the collections housed therein. In 1922 the *Yosemite Nature Notes* were first published, a monthly periodical devoted to items of interest in both the human and natural history of Yosemite. The last of Mather's proposals was realized in 1925 with the creation of the Yosemite School of Field Natural History, organized initially to answer the demand for more and better-trained guides for the Yosemite nature guide service.[22] This school operated successfully for many years before falling victim to general budgetary restrictions

Figure 50. Junior nature school, 1938.

brought about by the Second World War. Patronized at first mainly by California public school teachers the school also came to function as a training program for park naturalists in other national parks. The normal enrollment averaged about twenty students. In 1930 the Yosemite Junior Nature School was organized in which children of all ages were instructed in nature lore. Although it was maintained by some that the school was as much a baby-sitting service as institution of learning it was nevertheless popular enough to cause "several parents" to settle in Yosemite for the entire summer "because of the opportunity afforded their children."[23]

The emphasis upon nature studies that characterized the Yosemite of the 1920s found expression in many forms, from live animal exhibits of mountain lions and elk to flower shows featuring specimens of the local flora. A fish hatchery at Happy Isles served both as a supply of trout and an educational display of modern fish culture. For more than a decade a herd of Tule elk was displayed in an eight-foot wire-fenced paddock in the upper end of the Valley. Begun in 1921 with the introduction of six animals, the herd grew to a total of twenty-seven by 1933, when it was removed from the park for several reasons: one, the elk were an exotic species and didn't really belong there; and two, it was decided that the paddock was "unsightly" and the meadow enclosed therein was severely overgrazed.[24]

Perhaps the most popular "live animal" aspect of Yosemite nature interests concerned the park's bears. Prior to the 1920s bears were

Figure 51. Elk corral, Yosemite Valley.

infrequently seen in Yosemite. Visitors considered themselves fortunate to get even a fleeting glimpse of a bear, and they would commonly arouse all their neighbors when one came into view "so that they too might enjoy the experience."[25] The rapid increase of Yosemite visitors during the 1920s and the greatly increased amounts of garbage created resulted in a corresponding increase in the number of bears in the park, principally in the Valley. According to naturalist Harwell, before the thought of an incinerator in the Valley, garbage was dumped in great pits to be covered with earth. Night prowling bears discovered a new source of food. Night prowling tourists discovered a new source for bear observations. An alert traffic manager discovered a new source of revenue and soon park visitors were being transported to the "Bear Pit," armed with flashlights.[26] The first issue of *Yosemite Nature Notes*, dated July 10, 1922, declared that "many visitors to the Bear Pits have been well rewarded this year. At dusk or after dark is the time when they are usually seen, but this season they are even to be seen in broad daylight and are becoming very tame." Both to dignify this feeding and greater facilitate viewing by tourists, special platforms were built, electric lights installed, parking areas arranged, and larger and larger crowds assembled for the nightly bear shows and lectures. Caravans of automobiles gathered at the hotels to be led by a park ranger to the site of the evening's entertainment. Apparently the bears adjusted readily to this special feeding. An article in the *Yosemite Nature Notes* of June 7, 1924 reported that "although a few years ago

Figure 52. Bears at feeding platform, 1926.

Figure 53. Getting to know Mr. Bruin.

near approach was all that could be expected, this summer many (visitors) are having thrilling experiences having bears ... eat from their hands in their own camps."

At first Park Service officials were in favor of feeding the bears and providing lectures on their habits for the benefit of the tourists who, for the most part, were delighted over the opportunity to experience bruin on such an intimate basis. As things progressed, however, too many "thrilling" experiences turned into chilling ones; "bear accidents" began to increase at an alarming rate and for many visitors "intimate" contact with bruin produced considerably more pain than pleasure. Park rangers then attempted to discourage tourists from feeding and aggravating the bears but to no avail; an entire generation of Yosemite visitors had developed a habit that was difficult to break. Consequently, accidents became more frequent until finally more than sixty hospital cases were recorded during one season. Will Rogers, after a visit to Yosemite, observed that "they warn you not to feed the bears, but they have a hospital for those that do."[27] Yosemite bears finally became such a disruptive problem that in 1940 all feeding of bears in the Valley was discontinued. That autumn forty-five bears were trapped and removed to outlying areas in the park in the hope that their feeding habits would revert to a more natural state. Removal of bears from the Valley continued on an "as needed" basis until the "problem" was considered under control.

Another exhibit of "natural life" which flourished during this period was the "live" Indian exhibit behind the museum. Visitor interest in the Yosemite Indians had manifested itself in one form or another from the very first but with the diminishing numbers of natives had become relatively dormant. Perhaps the first real attempt to place the Indians in their proper perspective in Yosemite was the little book written by Galen Clark in 1904, *Indians of the Yosemite Valley and Vicinity*. On a more academic level was the chapter by A. L. Kroeber, Professor of Anthropology at the University of California, in Ansel Hall's *Handbook of Yosemite National Park* in 1921. In the enthusiasm for natural history that pervaded the 1920s Park Service officials felt it desirable that some sort of exhibit of Yosemite aboriginal life be presented to the interested public. Hence, in 1929 park naturalist Harwell worked out an agreement with several Piute Indians to demonstrate native crafts in an area behind the museum. Billed by the National Park Service as a top nature attraction, the Indian exhibit proved to be a popular feature with Yosemite visitors until its temporary demise in the 1940s.

Figure 54. Demonstrating Indian crafts, 1931.

Figure 55. Auto caravan tour of Yosemite Valley.

The nature interpretation program became one of Yosemite's most popular visitor attractions. Just two years after its inception it was estimated that approximately 73,000 visitor contacts were made, against a total of only slightly over 100,000 total park attendance. By the mid-twenties Mather jubilantly reported to the secretary of the Interior that "in the Yosemite National Park it is estimated that the nature guide service last year served two out of every three of the park's 209,166 visitors."[28] The number of visitors so served during the next few years continued to be approximately 60 percent of the total park attendance, with the museum being the single most attractive feature. (Data for bear lectures was not recorded.)

As the National Park Service approached the end of its first decade of existence it was apparent that profound changes were being wrought throughout the system. National parks were increasingly perceived as the nation's premier outdoor vacation sites, managed by a cooperative federal government to include a remarkable variety of scenic and recreational attractions. In the Yosemite the changes that accompanied the Park Service era, with the possible exception of the nature guide service, tended to reinforce existing visitor traditions rather than to introduce new ones. Even in the case of the nature guide service it can be argued that the program was as much an institutionalization of the interpretive legacy of Starr King, James Hutchings, David Curry, and John Muir and the Sierra Club as it was an innovation brought about by Park Service officials. Without belaboring the point, in Yosemite, perhaps more than in any other park, the notion of the national park as an outdoor vacation paradise achieved its fullest expression. In Yosemite the efforts of Mather and the Park Service to promote that notion were amply illustrated by the increasing diversity of the visitor experience. An analysis of that experience in terms of visitor behavior and preferences sheds light on visitor perception and utilization of the Yosemite landscape during the first decades of the National Park Service era.

Despite construction of the Ahwahnee Hotel and expansion of the Valley's various cabin and hotel camps most of Yosemite's visitors at any one time chose to patronize the park's free public campgrounds. During the 1920s it was not at all uncommon for the Valley's public campgrounds to accommodate between five and seven thousand persons per night, compared to a total of 2,800 in the Valley's combined hotels and hotel camps. Moreover, in contrast to patrons of commercial establishments many campers "settled" into the Valley's campgrounds for much of the summer. While at first such longevity of stay was seen as a symbol of Yosemite's growing success as a tourist attraction, it later became something of a problem. In 1935 officials imposed a thirty-day limit on camping in the Valley's five campgrounds. Although this restriction was unpopular at first, most Yosemite campers came to concede the necessity of such a policy; by the latter 1930s it appeared that the average length of stay for campers in the Valley had dropped to about seven days.[29]

During the great outdoors era, when camping first became fashionable, tourists were attracted to the sport supposedly because it provided opportunities for participants to "get close to nature" in a popular and virile way. By the 1920s both the motivation and manner of camping in the national parks were undergoing change. Campers were becoming less concerned with the primitive aspects of camping and more interested in camping as "an economical means of traveling about the country, of seeing the sights that formerly were available only to the well-to-do."[30] The economic advantages of camping were as apparent to Yosemite visitors as to anyone else, perhaps even more so since so many of the park's campers were Californians who made camping in Yosemite an annual event. Attendance figures from the early 1930s suggested that over half of the Valley's campers were "repeaters." Their average was slightly over three visits per year to the Yosemite country.[31]

As the motivation for going camping changed so did the manner in which campers enjoyed their sport. Campers were becoming less enamored with experiencing "naked reality" than in seeking a camp that was almost as convenient as home. In the last analysis, according to a study of camper habits conducted by Ranger Lon Garrison in the 1930s, "good roads, piped water, and modern comfort stations (seemed) to outweigh the call of the wild in most campers' minds." Campers were also less inclined than before to engage in many of the activities that traditionally had been associated with camping. Former- ly, for example, the communal spirit of sitting around an evening campfire, talking, singing, and telling stories was considered "one of the prime advantages of going camping." Not so any more, according to Garrison. Instead of providing their own entertainment around the warmth and conviviality of their own campfire, most campers, if they chose anything of the kind of an evening, tended to frequent the campfire lectures sponsored by the Park Service or the rather more professional entertainments offered by the commercial estab-

Figure 56. The rigors of camp life. Stoneman Meadow, 1927.

Figure 57. Camping and picnicing, Yosemite Valley, 1927.

Figure 58. Early camp trailer.

lishments. In doing so, noted Garrison somewhat sardonically, they conformed "with modern social trends which do not give much emphasis to self entertainment in the evening, or any other time."[32]

If campers, in their choice of discretionary activities, seemed increasingly distracted by alternatives less traditional to camping, they were but small cogs on a large wheel, a wheel whose dimensions and directions largely had been defined by the concessioners and the National Park Service. For when asked to identify those attractions that influenced them to choose campgrounds in the Valley over those in the backcountry, the choices cited by campers were an accurate expression of the very kinds of activities Yosemite managers had been promoting for an entire generation of Yosemite visitors: in descending order, more diversified recreation for all the family, more conveniences, a more extensive naturalist program, better recreation provided specifically for children, and more social contact with others, including proximity to other campers and the ever-popular evening dances at the pavilion.[33]

Despite the increased comforts of "modern" camping, the majority of Yosemite's annual visitors chose to patronize one of the park's commercial accommodations. These ranged in type from the wooden-floored tents of Camp Curry to the snobbish elegance of the Ahwahnee and included, in between, the small wooden bungalows of Yosemite

Figure 59. Evening campfire program in Camp 15.

Lodge, the several structures that made up the venerable Sentinel Hotel, the imposingly sited Glacier Point Hotel, the small Big Trees Lodge, the Tuolumne Meadows Lodge, and the several commercial tent camps that were scattered across the central High Sierra portion of the park. While most of Yosemite's middle class visitors stayed at Camp Curry it was the Ahwahnee Hotel that attracted the wealthiest of the park's clientele. When the Ahwahnee opened for business in 1927 it represented the culmination of more than sixty years effort to establish a truly first class resort hotel within the confines of Yosemite Valley. Prior to that time a commonly voiced criticism was that "there was no place in the Yosemite for a man of means." In the opinion of one guidebook author the Yosemite had become a camper's park, there not being a hotel of sufficient quality to attract the tourist of taste. He regretted that in the minds of many European and American travelers "the mountain scenery of Western America is a scenery of mere savage bigness, rather than of predominant beauty." In his opinion such a complaint "will be forgotten (only) with the multiplication of expensive hotels."[34]

The Gilded Age tourist was far from extinct among contemporary travelers. Indeed, despite his relative decline numerically, the traditionally wealthy and fashion conscious traveler so typical of the romantic era continued to exert a degree of influence in Yosemite far out of proportion to his numbers. It was this type of tourist that the Ahwahnee was designed to attract. Everything about the establishment, from its high prices to its policy prohibiting "gentlemen" entrance to the dining room unless properly attired in coats and ties, catered to that segment of society accustomed "to the delights of luxurious living, and to whom the artistic excellence and the material comforts of their environment is important."[35] In terms of its "artistic excellence" and "material comforts" the Ahwahnee was advertised as something more than a hotel. "Its feeling is that of a spacious house whose owner has planned it boldly but with faultless instinct." In essence the general atmosphere and facilities of the Ahwahnee were ample evidence of the fact that elitism was still very much a part of the perception and utilization of the Yosemite landscape. Efforts by management to promote the Ahwahnee version of the Yosemite experience appealed directly to travelers accustomed to frequenting pleasure resorts known as much for their exclusiveness as for their fashionability.

In terms of its patron orientation and its carefully landscaped grounds the Ahwahnee was a world within a world, a social enclave reminiscent of an earlier generation of national park use. In no case was this exclusivity better expressed than by the barbed wire-topped chain link fence which separated the hotel grounds from adjacent campgrounds, thereby assuring Ahwahnee guests their purchased privacy. While publicity surrounding the Ahwahnee was generally favorable there were some, nevertheless, who pointed out inconsistencies between the national park idea and what the Ahwahnee represented. Decrying the Ahwahnee as a "millionaire's palace," a California physician suggested that it was a terrible "mistake to flaunt so boldly the luxury and profligacy of the millionaire class before the gaze of the unwashed thousands who come to Yosemite in their flivvers to enjoy the simple life in the bosom of nature. Too big a contrast!" Dr. Kylberg went on to point out that "Mr. Mather and the Department of the Interior should not have allowed such unbridled luxury in Yosemite. It causes the restless to be more restless."[36]

In Yosemite the emphasis upon outdoor recreation continued to be a principal ingredient of the contemporary visitor experience. The traditional outdoor sports of camping, hiking, and fishing were augmented by the introduction of golf, tennis, and dancing as managers sought to provide for their guests all the expressions of outdoor recreation usually associated with vacation resorts. Especially characteristic

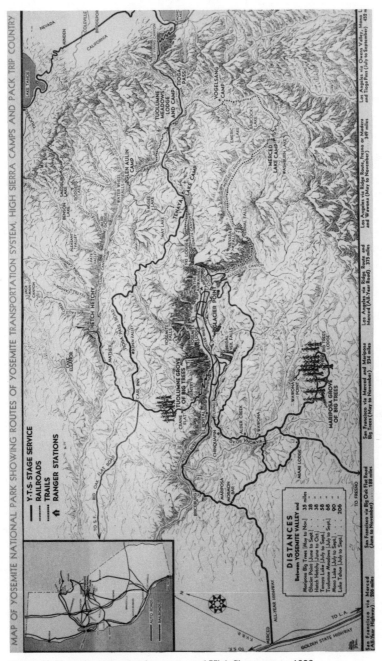

Figure 60. Yosemite transportation routes and High Sierra camps, 1938.

of this period, perhaps, was the growing utilization of the High Sierra and the popularization, especially during the 1930s, of winter sports. The opening up of the High Sierra for increased visitor use became something of an obsession with Mather and his associates. By the 1924 season a half dozen "hikers' camps" had been established with several more in the planning stages. Similar camps had already proven popular in the White Mountains of New Hampshire, where the Appalachian Mountain Club had developed a series of huts that dated back to the early 1900s. Offering food and shelter, these huts were acclaimed as offering hikers an "interesting walk of from three to seven days . . . without the incumberance of the carrying of blankets or provisions."[37] The provision of such accommodations was not considered a dilution of the hiking and camping experience. Rather it was seen as a means whereby greater numbers of people of less than herculean stamina could come to know and love the beauties of the High Country. As Ansel Hall put it, "Hikers' camps are not intended for 'dudes' (hotel-bound tourists). They were opened for those who wish to get away from the overcrowded tourist centers and live with the vastness of the big country."[38]

Even with the opening of the High Sierra Camps, as they came to be called, pressure continued to mount for the development of the High Sierra for greater visitor use. An interesting and revealing comment to this effect was that of Mather's successor as director of the National Park Service, Horace Albright. As part of Albright's annual report of 1929 he argued that if Yosemite was to contribute its full value to the nation and justify California's faith in giving it into federal control, the high country "must be made more accessible by the improvement of roads, by better trails, by much better fishing, by more high country camps, by the extension of the naturalist and ranger services, by the safeguarding of water supplies, by the erection of log lean-to shelters, and other appropriate devices that will encourage the use of this superlative high country and yet not develop to the point of destroying virginal quality."[39] (Clearly Albright's ideas of "appropriate" developments and what constituted the "point of destroying virginal quality" differed greatly from those of subsequent generations.) What mattered at the time, though, was that the High Sierra backcountry portion of the park was perceived as relatively undeveloped. Given the fact that Yosemite Valley was increasingly perceived as overcrowded, it was probably natural that park managers should view the High Sierra not only as an opportunity for hikers to enjoy a superlative outdoor experience but also as a means of relieving visitor pressure in the Valley.

No group was more vocal in its advocacy of the High Sierra than members of the Sierra Club. In their sure knowledge that theirs was a higher form of nature experience Sierrans often looked with disdain on "those whom we might have been tempted to call weaker brethren, who venture no farther than this (the Valley) into the Sierra. Yet one feels a little sorry for them, for what do they know?"[40] Other outing participants were less kind; after experiencing a day's layover in the Valley prior to ascending into the High Sierra one Charles Noble wrote that "to a Sierran bound for the high mountains the human noise and dust of Yosemite (Valley) seem desecration of primitive nature." He went on to suggest that his "wait-over of twenty-four hours in this anomaly of automobiles and silks" could be regarded, at best, only as a "necessary evil."[41] If there was one characteristic of Sierra Club members, other than a general interest in the outdoors, that bound them together as a group it was that they shared the conviction that the "true" Yosemite experience could no longer be enjoyed within the confines of the Valley. Only in the more expansive and primitive context of the High Sierra, they maintained, was it possible to experience nature in the Yosemite in the manner prescribed by the immortal John Muir.

While the construction of the Badger Pass facility drew most formal winter sports activities away from the Valley, in at least one case the Valley became the scene of one of the most enduring of Yosemite's winter attractions. On the evening of December 25 the Yosemite Park and Curry Company staged a special Christmas feast after the order of the dinner described by Washington Irving in "The Sketch Book." Known as the Bracebridge Hall Dinner, this gala occasion was staged in the Ahwahnee Hotel, where President and Mrs. Tresidder assumed the parts of Squire Bracebridge and his wife. Costumed in the guise of the period, guests enjoyed the traditional menu which included "the Boar's Head, the Baron of Beef, the Fish, the Peacock Pie, the Flaming Pudding, and the Wassail Bowl brought into a special setting as in the days of old."[42] During and after the feast company employees—in costume—provided musical entertainment in the form of "old carols and wakes." One of the most talented and imaginative of these entertainers was the musically-inclined Ansel Adams, whose legacy to the Yosemite would someday be based more on his skill as a photographic artist than a musician. The Bracebridge Hall Dinner came to be one of

Figure 61. Bracebridge dinner, Ahwahnee Hotel, 1928.

Yosemite's most famous winter attractions, serving for many years as the highlight of the park's winter social season.

In addition to hiking and camping and winter sports the contemporary Yosemite visitor experience involved a rather remarkable variety of other recreational activities. While some of these had been popular in the park for some time, others were introduced during the 1920s and illustrate well the extent to which outdoor recreation was emphasized in the national parks. Fishing for sport was an activity that had become popular among the vacationing classes during the nineteenth century when it was introduced from Europe as a "gentleman's" sport. Prior to that time most fishing in Yosemite was done either by the Indians or others employed by hotel owners to provide food for the table. Mather himself was an avid fisherman and in his enthusiastic way maintained that the Yosemite National Park was a "fisherman's paradise, especially in the High Sierra country." To insure the perpetuity thereof he promoted the construction of fish hatcheries and the stocking of the park's lakes and streams so that "each body of water in the park should be made productive."[43] In Hall's *Handbook of Yosemite National Park* fishing is extolled as one of the chief attractions of the park. One of the chief attractions of the handbook, at least so far as fishermen were concerned, was an appendix in

Figure 62. Winter Carnival at Camp Curry, 1932.

the back of the book that listed the lakes and streams of Yosemite, the species of fish that lived therein, and the quality of the fishing. By the middle 1920s the daily catch limit had been reduced to twenty-five; prior to that time fishermen caught and kept pretty much according to their "luck," particularly where table-fishing was concerned.

The recreation-resort atmosphere of Yosemite was promoted by Park Service and concessioner officials alike. For instance, Director Mather felt that a small golf course needed to be built on the grounds of the Ahwahnee for those too old or otherwise unfit to enjoy more rigorous outdoor sports. In this respect he was more than supported by Yosemite Superintendent Charles Thomson, an avid golfer in his own right. In the annual report to the secretary of the Interior, Mather's successor, Horace Albright, reported in 1930 that "a small pitch-and-putt golf course made an attractive addition to the Ahwahnee grounds."[44]

In his enthusiasm for promoting all kinds of recreational attractions Yosemite Park & Curry Company president Donald Tresidder was a worthy counterpart of Stephen Mather. Under his leadership the company sponsored a variety of activities that would "raise the hair" of park management officials of later generations. Among these was the "firedive," a Yosemite Lodge alternative to the firefall. The firedive consisted of a diver who set his costume on fire immediately prior to making a swan dive into the Lodge swimming pool. Other attractions were less dramatic and ranged from the Indian Field Days activity begun by Mother Curry to wildflower festivals and historical pageants that celebrated the pioneer tradition in Yosemite. One time during the 1920s Mother Curry felt that it would be an interesting addition to the firefall to have fireworks displayed on top of Half Dome. In compliance with her wishes several employees packed eighty pounds of fireworks to the top and strung them across the face of the Dome.[45]

Recreation-resort activities were not restricted to the Valley or its immediate surroundings. For several years during the 1920s the Merced Lake High Sierra camp was operated as a sports-oriented boys camp complete with two tennis courts, two basketball courts, and a baseball diamond. Rounding out the recreational attractions of the camp were the more traditional outdoor sports of fishing, swimming, boating, hiking, and horseback riding. The camp even came equipped with its own psychiatrist. After 1926 the Curry Company operated the camp and expanded it in size. At the time it was the only camp to boast hot-and-cold showers and canvas cabins with permanent floors, a fact which contributed substantially to its great popularity with long-staying guests.[46]

One of the most significant characteristics of the inter-war era visitor experience was the tremendous increase in automobile use. The popularity of autocamping as a form of outdoor recreation was indicated by the estimate in 1922 that half of the automobiles on the road in America were used for camping.[47] Driving was seen as a skill to be perfected in its own right, while autocamping, with all its paraphernalia and regimen, came to be practiced almost as much as an art form as a means of diversion. Motor touring, with its greater economy, easy sociability, and tremendously greater versatility, also appealed to the growing number of middle class Americans who were taking to the highways each summer. This was the group that came to dominate the Yosemite scene of the 1920s and 1930s. In response to publicity from both the National Park Service and the private business world they came to the Yosemite in search of a vacation experience that was complex in nature but only partly related to the uniqueness of the Yosemite landscape. To many of these motor tourists Yosemite was but one of several destinations that combined opportunities for sightseeing with the pleasures and satisfactions to be obtained from automobile travel. In this context we can better understand the oft-maligned

Figure 63. Ruth St. Dennis, pageant player.

motorists of the period who seemed "contented to stare about them for a day or two, expend a few expletives, snap a camera at this and that, and anon be off again."[48]

The lure of nature lore had been a part of Yosemite's tourist heritage since the days when landlord Peck and J. S. Hutchings entertained their guests around the evening fireplace with their opinions of how the Yosemite country was formed. It was under the tutelage of the national park ranger, however, that nature interpretation became such a popular and integral aspect of the contemporary national park experience. In the minds of the vacationing public, "the ranger was one of the most romantic figures in life."[49] In him was envisioned the very

113

Figure 64. Yosemite Chief Ranger Forest Townsley welcomes automobilist, 1923.

ultimate in national park values. Host, guide, guardian, and interpreter, he seemed to reflect all the best attributes of intelligence, woodsmanship, and rugged strength that had romanticized the entire history of the Western movement. He was the very epitome of all that nature could bring out in a man. To the national park enthusiast the ranger led an idyllic life; surrounded by the beauty and majesty of the mountains, forests, and streams, his was an existence unsullied by the pettiness of the mundane workaday world.

If the ranger came to epitomize the romantic image of the national parks, the bears in turn provided the comic relief. Bears became a virtual Yosemite institution as tourists teased, fed, and photographed the apparently tame beasts. The more cautious of Yosemite's bear fans usually did their observing and feeding from the comparative safety of their automobiles; the more cautious among these even took out bear insurance policies on their machines! It was largely in the attempt to localize bear feeding and lure the animals out of the campgrounds that the National Park Service began the bear feeding program at the local garbage pits.

Subsequent historians of national park policy have been critical of the "zoo" attitude toward wildlife that characterized the inter-war period. It should be pointed out, however, that Mather, Albright, & "company" reflected attitudes which were prevalent among nature enthusiasts of the time. To Albright, in particular, wild animals con-

Figure 65. The Gilmore economy run, 1940.

stituted one of the chief attractions of the national parks. While assistant director of the Park Service and superintendent of Yellowstone he encouraged a variety of wildlife displays, from the so-called Buffalo corral at Mammoth Hot Springs to the cages wherein were kept for the convenience of interested viewers deer, elk, coyotes, bears, porcupines, and badgers.[50] Albright especially enjoyed bears and it was largely from his personal collection of bear anecdotes that the popular book *"Oh, Ranger!"* was compiled. Bears became the subjects for numerous books, magazine articles, and even movies, ranging from the children's stories of Thornton W. Burgess to the enormously popular cinematic works of Walt Disney. The tendency to view animal life in anthropomorphic terms was characteristic of the age. When visitors to national parks sought opportunities to experience wildlife on a personal basis they were exhibiting behavior that was as normal as it was enjoyable. Indeed, it was probably true that for many national park visitors the exposure to wild animals constituted the most memorable attraction of their park experience.

The year 1926 marked the end of the first decade of the National Park Service's existence as an official government agency. By all accounts it had been a fruitful one. Under the dynamic leadership of Stephen Mather the national parks had emerged as one of this country's unique and most successful institutions. Contemporary perceptions of the parks were twofold: one, in their function as the

Figure 66. Forest Townsley, left, preparing for a pack trip.

"nation's playgrounds" the parks offered a tremendous opportunity to enjoy a multi-faceted vacation experience in the most magnificent of natural settings; and two, under the aegis of the Park Service's nature interpretation programs the national parks did much to crystallize in the minds of the vacationing public the relationship of nature to the American way of life. Aided by the mushrooming use of the automobile the number of people visiting the parks each year continued to soar at a rate that taxed the ability of park management officials to provide for them. Heady with the successes of its first decade of achievements, the National Park Service continued its policies of development and popularization throughout the second. Following the premature death of Mather in 1930, these policies were continued by his successors who, for the most part, shared his philosophies of national park use and management.

Mather's relationship to Yosemite National Park had been both personal and unique. A true Californian at heart, he had long considered Yosemite his "favorite park." Furthermore, he felt that in Yosemite the national park experience had achieved its happiest expression. In his efforts to develop a nation-wide park system he utilized Yosemite as a "model park" and urged other park administrators to follow its example.[51] There is no evidence to suggest that he was anything but pleased with what he considered the "successes" of Yosemite. To the contrary, exulting over the "thousands of happy vacationists" that "thronged" the park each summer he maintained

Figure 67. Yosemite Junior Nature School and visitor, 1930.

that Yosemite had "attained a new record of usefulness in the life of the nation."[52] In noting that Yosemite had achieved stature as a "winter as well as a summer resort" he proclaimed an accomplishment that reflected years of dedicated effort.

Mather took great pride in the physically and morally regenerative aspects of the national park experience. "The function of the parks as factors increasing our national health, vitality, and happiness is a most important one. To encourage clean living in God's great out-of-doors should be one of the primary ideals of the Service." Ever the confirmed nationalist, Mather went on to point out that "the European visitor whose ideal vacation so often consists in lounging about a hotel and viewing nature from the veranda, marvels at the number of people he finds hiking, riding, swimming, or otherwise engaged in strenuous sports in the Yosemite." While extolling the virtues of the more rigorous forms of outdoor recreation he nevertheless recognized the fact that there were those "who required 'artificial' amusements" and that there would "always be entertainments, dancing, bowling, pool, etc., at the larger hotels, camps, and lodges." Such development caused Mather little concern. After all, as discussed earlier, he had dedicated his entire career as a professional national parks man to the development of the parks as vacation opportunities designed to appeal to the widest possible spectrum of visitors. In his own words, he maintained that "the ideal of each individual member of the Service and of the Service itself is to give to the public not merely what they pay for, but everything within power."[53] In his typically direct way, his successor put it even more bluntly by stating that in the national parks "everybody gets what he wants. That is the national park policy."[54]

To subsequent generations of national parks people this unabashed "give them whatever they want" policy has been a source of considerable embarrassment. In a study of visitor habits written in the 1960s a future Park Service professional was critical of the degree to which his predecessors had catered to what he felt were inappropriate developments in Yosemite. Although his criticisms were directed toward the Yosemite scene of 1913 they could have applied equally to that of the 1920s or 1930s.

Figure 68. From a 1925 Yosemite Park and Curry Company brochure.

In a more subtle and subjective vein the 'mood' of the park also suffered. Concessionaires and government agencies alike contributed to the emphasis of the playground and entertainment atmosphere of the Park to the detriment of the aesthetic and inspirational values associated with a visit to a primitive area. The government dance pavilion and Curry's swimming pool, dance facility, and Firefall were not necessary to enjoy Half Dome, Yosemite Falls, or the wildlife. The cultural landscape of 1913 did not reflect man's finest hour.[55]

In condemning an earlier generation's "emphasis" upon a "playground and entertainment atmosphere" the above author fell prey to a tendency only too common among historians and interpreters of the national parks movement. In their concern for an evolving conservation ethic they have overlooked the importance of contemporary needs and perceptions. When Mather assumed directorship of the newly-created National Park Service he was keenly aware of the

Figure 69. From a 1930s Yosemite Park and Curry Company brochure.

uncertain status of the parks with regard to preservation and use policies. He felt strongly that in order to survive threats of exploitation by timber, mining, and water interests the national parks needed the support of a large percentage of the American public. In his judgement the best way of obtaining that support was to make the parks an attractive and rewarding vacation possibility for the widest possible spectrum of the traveling public.

Rightly or wrongly, most of his peers agreed with his judgement. In their enthusiasm to foster visitor satisfaction by meeting tourist demands park management people at times seemed unconcerned with the potential impact of such development upon park resources. "But these resources did not seem threatened in 1935," wrote ex-ranger Lon Garrison in 1983, "and in reality—coinciding with the great conservation theme which the rangers and the park leadership shared—much of the park management favored not developing protective skills, but establishing ways and means to welcome and to serve more and more people."[56] As stated by another Yosemite ranger in the 1920s, "The policy of the National Park Service in making the Park 'liveable' and more and more accessible is unquestionably the right one."[57] Contemporary Park Service officials were pragmatic in their approach to attracting visitors. They understood well that many tourists able to afford vacation travel sought nature only in moderation, and rather than resenting the conveniences of the resorts with their contrived attractions, luxury hotels, and ease of access by railroad or highway, they preferred such as places at which to spend a vacation. With regard to a search for wilderness values, "for most tourists, the quest for nature was an inclination to pleasure, and not a dedication to truly profound comprehension."[58]

As the tempo of national park activity slowed during the Great Depression, only to be brought to a near-halt by the outbreak of World War II, the curtain was drawn on another generation of Yosemite tourism. For better or for worse, Yosemite had emerged as a popular, year-round vacation resort. Visitor perception during this period had been affected by a number of factors, chief among them the efforts of the National Park Service and concessioners to attract and satisfy increasing numbers of tourists. That such efforts were successful was amply evidenced by the number of visitors who chose to spend their summer vacations in the Yosemite; for many of those a trip to Yosemite had become an annual event. The strongly developed sense of mission that had characterized service employees since Mather's day was strongly felt throughout the system, and despite the fiscal problems associated with the Depression years there were some who, in fact, did feel that the Yosemite experience of the 1920s and 1930s represented the park's "finest hour" as a great national institution.

> We would venture to suggest what cannot be substantiated and must remain a subjective statement, that the period 1935-1940 was in the nature of a peak of both achievement and enjoyment. Morale in the service was very high and the visitors found it possible to gain that experience of a national park which had been the ideal of the pioneers of the movement.[59]

Stated in another way, one in which Stephen Mather, David Curry, and Donald Tresidder most likely would have taken great satisfaction, was this comment by a contemporary tourist. "Yosemite is a genial host, full of good-nature, indulgent, happy to see his guests enjoy life on their own terms, even though (that) enjoyment has a ring of triviality about it."[60] More than any other single statement, this describes the perceptions and utilizations of the Yosemite country of the inter-war period.

Figure 70. A young snowshoer.

Chapter 6
The Wilderness Era

TRAVEL TO THE NATIONAL PARKS fell off sharply during the Second World War. Even in Yosemite, with its relatively near-by population base, visitation dropped below 117,000 in 1943, the lowest figure since 1924 and less than one-fifth the immediately pre-war figure of 600,000. By the latter 1940s, however, the hiatus in visitation came to an abrupt end and the number of people frequenting the parks resumed its upward climb. As a matter of fact, long before demobilization was completed the rate of visitor increase to national parks was soaring at an unprecedented rate. The annual number of visitors to Yosemite had not reached the half-million mark until 1940, eighty-five years after its beginning as a tourist attraction. Less than fifteen years later this figure had doubled—during 1954 over one million persons visited the park. Only little more than a decade later the figure had doubled again, to more than two million in 1967, with no apparent slow-down in sight.

The phenomenal increase in Yosemite and other national park travel coincided with a nation-wide surge in the popularity of outdoor recreation and tourism. The growth and prosperity of the 1950s was accompanied by ever-increasing amounts of leisure time among the populace as a whole. Anxious to enjoy their affluence, millions of Americans took to the outdoors to spend their vacation time and dollars. Such efforts were facilitated greatly by the large-scale construction of high-speed, limited access interstate highways. With the "freeway" came the four hundred and five hundred mile per day family vacation trip which made it possible for increasing numbers of Americans—the majority of whom still lived east of the Mississippi—to visit the country's great legacy of scenic outdoor recreation landscapes—most of which were located in the mountainous western half of the country.

For the most part the nation was ill-prepared to meet the rapidly accelerating demand for additional sites and facilities. In an attempt to assess the situation and to make recommendations for the future, the Outdoor Recreation Resources Review Commission was established in 1958. The first large-scale study of its type, it did much both to identify specific needs and to chart plans for future developments. Throughout the next two decades a tremendous growth was to occur in all sorts of outdoor recreation facilities as state and federal agencies, along with a variety of private interests, attempted to satisfy the national passion for the outdoors.

The rapidly expanding popularity of the national parks, unfortunately, was not accompanied by a commensurate increase in either appropriations or personnel. The virtual dearth in wartime funding had left the parks in a sad state of neglect. Despite the post-war return to peace and prosperity, Congress seemed little disposed to appropriate the funds necessary to restore the parks even to their pre-war level of operation. According to director Conrad Wirth, the situation was such that the National Park Service was not able to provide even "essential

Figure 71. Tourist Travel to Yosemite, 1855–1987.

1855	42	1903	8,376	1931	461,855	1959	1,061,471
1855–64	653	1904	9,500	1932	498,289	1960	1,150,385
1864	147	1905	10,103	1933[6]	296,088	1961	1,227,110
1865	369	1906[3]	5,414	1934	309,431	1962	1,505,496
1866	438	1907	7,102	1935	372,317	1963	1,473,400
1867	502	1908	8,850	1936	431,192	1964	1,547,034
1868	623	1909	13,182	1937	481,492	1965	1,635,380
1869[1]	1,122	1910	13,619	1938	443,325	1966	1,817,060
1870	1,735	1911	12,530	1939	466,552	1967[7]	2,201,484
1871	2,137	1912	10,884	1940	506,781	1968	2,281,077
1872	2,354	1913[4]	12,255	1941	594,062	1969	2,291,329
1873	2,530	1914	15,154	1942	332,550	1970	2,277,193
1874	2,711	1915	31,546	1943	127,643	1971	2,416,380
1875	2,423	1916	33,398	1944	119,515	1972	2,266,634
1876	1,917	1917	34,510	1945	251,931	1973	2,339,427
1877	1,392	1918	35,527	1946	641,767	1974	2,343,123
1878	1,183	1919	58,362	1947	775,878	1975	2,619,042
1879	1,385	1920	68,906	1948	749,861	1976	2,753,142
1880	1,897	1921	91,513	1949	802,572	1977	2,535,846
1881	2,173	1922	100,506	1950	830,241	1978	2,669,200
1882	2,525	1923	481,492	1951	850,585	1979	2,441,385
1883	2,831	1924	146,070	1952	963,536	1980	2,583,154
1884	2,408	1925	209,166	1953	969,225	1981	2,616,260
1885	2,590	1926[5]	274,209	1954	1,008,031	1982	2,506,241
1886–99[2]		1927	490,430	1955	984,201	1983	2,549,499
1899	4,500	1928	460,619	1956	1,114,173	1984	2,842,942
1900–01[2]		1929	461,257	1957	1,138,716	1985	2,939,436
1902	8,023	1930	458,566	1958	1,139,343	1986	2,982,758
						1987	3,266,342

(1) Overland railroad completed. (2) No travel record was kept. (3) San Francisco earthquake and fire. (4) Private automobiles admitted to park. (5) Merced River Canyon all-weather road completed. (6) Counting procedure changed. (7) Counting procedure changed again; comparisons with previous years cannot be made.

Source: NPS, Yosemite National Park.

services." Visitor concentration points could not be kept in sanitary condition. Comfort stations couldn't be kept clean and serviced. Water, sewer, and electrical systems were taxed to the utmost. Protective services to safeguard the public and preserve park values were far short of requirements. Physical facilities were either deteriorating or inadequate to meet public needs. "Some of the camps," he warned, "are approaching rural slums. We actually get scared when we think of the bad health conditions."[1]

In Yosemite, as in other national parks, the crisis posed by the post-war visitation surge affected Park Service and concessioner personnel alike. In the face of increasingly heavy use pressures tourist facilities of all kinds proved to be inadequate. Under-staffed and antiquated facilities had deteriorated to conditions substantially inferior to their pre-war level. What appropriations a niggardly Congress saw fit to bestow fell desperately short of the park's needs. According to one account underpaid rangers and their families were forced to live in shacks, old barns, barracks, and even a former slaughterhouse. Concessioner-operated facilities fared little better. With the exception of the Ahwahnee, Yosemite's hotels were old and sorely in need of renovation. Even the concessioner's "favored son" had served as a navy rehabilitation hospital during the war and needed extensive reconditioning to restore it to its former state.

Despite inadequate facilities within Yosemite and other national parks, visitors continued to come in increasing numbers, taxing existing facilities far beyond their capacities. As conditions worsened the public outcry grew in intensity and volume. Well-known and widely respected authors wrote scathingly about the deplorable state of the parks. Much of the criticism was directed toward a penurious Congress, whose fiscal irresponsibility led one writer to the conclusion that "much of the priceless heritage which the Service must safeguard for the United States is beginning to go to hell."[2]

In an effort to respond to the crisis, the National Park Service produced a comprehensive plan entitled "Mission 66." Conceived in the development-prone spirit of the times, Mission 66 was intended to be an intensive, long-range assessment of national park conditions, problems, and objectives, as well as a plan that would direct park development through the coming decades. The name of the program reflected the plan's principal objective of meeting the projected visitation estimates for the year 1966. Of paramount importance, from the pragmatically minded Park Service viewpoint, was the question of how to deal with the mushrooming numbers of visitors that were arriving at the parks each year. Given the decade or so of neglect, no matter what else Mission 66 might mean to future park management, visitor facilities of all types demanded immediate attention if only for reasons of health and safety.

In Yosemite one of the primary objectives of Mission 66 was to determine how far the National Park Service wanted to go in providing for the park's increasing crowds of tourists. Park Service officials were well aware of complaints from some of Yosemite's old-time visitors that the Valley, in particular, was becoming "horribly overcrowded"—a complaint, by the way, that had been more or less chronic since the 1870s. Consequently, the determination of a visitor "ceiling" in the Valley was considered to be among the first of the major post-war problems to be tackled. Based on deliberation of past experience park planners concluded that "a ceiling of about 8,000 campers and 4,500 concessioner-provided accommodations is considered to be the limit." With this ceiling in mind the basic objectives developed along three lines: first, the modification or modernization of visitor facilities in the Valley and maintenance of the established ceiling; second, the removal of all but absolutely necessary operating facilities from the Valley; and third, the development of accommodations, facilities, and services in other sections of the park to relieve over-crowding, but at the same time permit quick and easy access by car to the Valley and its renowned scenic features.

The first of these objectives was facilitated by the completion of the new Yosemite Lodge, a sprawling composite of central buildings and outlying sleeping quarters, the "modification and modernization" of other concessioner accommodations, and the construction and expansion of the Valley Visitor Center, campground sanitation facilities, and a smaller visitor center at Happy Isles. The second envisioned the removal to the El Portal area of such items as an "obsolete incinerator, the dump near Camp 11, warehouses, bulk storage, repair shops, certain employee housing, and related supporting facilities of the National Park Service and Yosemite concessioners."[3] The third objective involved the construction of facilities outside the Valley which, it was hoped, would relieve tourist pressure therein by creating competition in other areas of the park. This goal took shape in the form of improved access roads into the High Sierra, the construction of new and enlargement of old campgrounds and picnic areas, and the construction of the Yosemite Pioneer History Center at Wawona.

Figure 72. General store, Old Village, 1946.

In Yosemite, as throughout most of the national park system, the basic objectives of Mission 66 were to "wipe out the accumulated deficiencies, to project a ten-year plan, and to protect the parks as we presumed Mather and Albright would have done."[4] In many respects the program was lauded as an "extraordinary success." By the latter 1960s National Park Service Historian Ronald F. Lee described Mission 66 as a "magnificent concept, timed with great skill, and conducted with energy, foresight and unusual professional talent."[5] Its chief drawback, which perhaps was not really its fault, was that it had underestimated the growing popularity of the parks among the American people. By 1966 the actual number of visitors to the national parks exceeded the estimates of Mission 66 planners by 53 million persons; the cost of the program had risen from the original estimate of $459 million to $659 million.

Despite falling short of its goal, Mission 66 brought resolution to problems which had vexed park management for years, particularly in the area of sanitation and employee housing. There were growing numbers of people, however, who were not convinced that the goals and accomplishments of Mission 66 represented the best interests of the national parks. Long before the projected target date of the program in 1966 complaints were rising from numerous sources that Mission 66 was, in fact, a travesty upon the "true" mission of the National Park Service, which was to preserve and protect rather than promote and develop. In their minds the guiding philosophy of Mission

Figure 73. Trailer living in Camp 6, 1949.

66—the entire Park Service, in fact—was altogether too "development-oriented" and far too little concerned with the preservation of the primary national park resource, the natural environment. The preference for preservation over use signalled a change in attitudes toward nature that would profoundly influence the ways that Americans perceived and utilized their natural landscapes.

For most of the nation's history it was generally accepted that development was a necessary prelude to growth, and that both were necessary ingredients of prosperity. The exploitation of nature's gifts, i.e., such natural resources as water, timber, and minerals, was seen as an integral component of the process. When such exploitation resulted in the modification or degradation of the natural environment, it was accepted as a necessary and therefore justifiable cost of progress. As long as the quest for material affluence dominated Americans' priorities there was little incentive to be concerned with whether or not that "cost" was, in fact, one that, in the long run, should or even could be paid.

By the middle years of the twentieth century there was a growing suspicion that the environmental cost of prosperity was no longer acceptable. An increasing body of evidence suggested that wanton abuse of the environment not only detracted from the quality of life but posed serious threats to life itself. Air and water pollutants were elevated from the status of public nuisances to the level of health hazards as environmental factors were increasingly tied to such dreaded killers as cancer and heart disease. The importance of this latter fact can scarcely be over-stressed. Conservationists had been decrying the abuse of the environment since the latter nineteenth century without making a general impact upon the American lifestyle. Only when such abuse could be proven life-threatening did the public begin to get concerned. It seemed that only in times of crisis could the inertia of public opinion be surmounted and the concerns of the population be transformed into political action.

Proponents of the "new conservation" soon learned that the growing disillusionment with big business and even bigger government could be harnessed and translated into citizen activism. In this endeavor they were assisted immeasurably by the Vietnam War. Americans who initially saw the conflict as a nobly conceived attempt to protect freedom and democracy became increasingly cynical as the war progressed. Disenchantment festered into distrustful cynicism, and the idea of a corporate conspiracy against the common man and the simpler elements of "mother earth" became easier to swallow. Tactics of crisis confrontation were developed wherein issues that could be elevated to crisis proportions could be used to justify measures that were frequently extreme, often illegal, and sometimes violent. When such was the case it could be excused on the grounds that throughout their history the American people had been forced to resort to strong tactics in order to accomplish worthwhile objectives.

Of fundamental importance to the environmental movement was the assumption that technological man and the natural world were basically incompatible. In his headlong quest for material prosperity, modern man not only had demonstrated an astounding disregard for the natural environment but had totally alienated himself from the very essence of life. It was this essence that environmentalists sought to regain by seeking after that which was wild and unspoiled in nature. The quest for wealth was replaced by a search for wilderness as a new generation of Americans adopted the message of Thoreau, that "in wilderness is the preservation of the world."

The establishment in September 1964 of the National Wilderness Preservation System, referred to as the wilderness act, signalled the extent to which Americans had come to recognize and desire the benefits of undefiled nature. Such an act had been the dream of conservationists from the days of John Muir and represented the efforts of many to achieve formal recognition for wilderness. The act accomplished several important objectives. First among these was the problem of definition. It turned out to be surprisingly difficult to achieve agreement on what exactly constituted "wilderness." After prolonged debate legislators arrived at what would prove to be a reasonably workable definition of an extremely thorny phenomenon.

A wilderness, in contrast with those areas where man and his own works dominate the landscape, is hereby recognized as an area where the earth and its community of life are untrammeled by man, where man himself is a visitor who does not remain. An area of wilderness is further defined to mean in this Act an area of undeveloped Federal land retaining its primeval character and influence, without permanent improvements or human habitation, which is protected and managed so as to preserve its natural conditions and which (1) generally appears to have been affected primarily by the forces of nature, with the imprint of man's work substantially unnoticeable; (2) has outstanding opportunities for solitude or a primitive and unconfined type of recreation; (3) has at least five thousand acres of land or is of sufficient size as to make practicable its preservation and use in an unimpaired condition; and (4) may also contain ecological, geological, or other features of scientific, educational, scenic, or historical value.[6]

A second objective of the wilderness act involved the charge to federal land management agencies, such as the National Park Service and the National Forest Service, to study the lands under their jurisdiction and to make recommendations regarding parcels suitable for inclusion in the national wilderness system. This charge was not always appreciated by senior Park Service personnel, such as Lon Garrison, who maintained that the national park enabling legislation provided for adequate protection of wilderness lands within the system and did not require the complications of additional designation. While the actual process of redesignation would stretch on for decades, the philosophical intent of the wilderness act was felt more immediately, mainly in the form of downplaying development and removing from the parks things that were perceived to be "artificial" and not in keeping with the parks' value as wilderness.

Of fundamental and far-reaching importance was the shift away from the traditional notion that "parks were for people." In decided contrast to the days when Stephen Mather and Horace Albright encouraged Americans to enjoy national parks as outdoor playgrounds, wilderness-minded officials in the Department of the Interior adopted the slogan that national parks should be valued as "vignettes of pristine America." As such their scenic and natural curiosity value was to be superceded by their importance as preserves of primeval nature, wherein man and his activities were to be minimized, if not removed.

Such a pronounced change in philosophy did not always sit well with old-timers in the Park Service, who still adhered to the values and philosophies of the Mather era. Such resistance notwithstanding, wilderness philosophy came to dominate the thinking of professional Park Service personnel, particularly the younger generation.

Within the national park system, Yosemite was considered by wilderness advocates as the one park most at odds with the new philosophy. By the middle 1960s conditions in the Valley, in particular, were approaching the crisis stage. It was generally acknowledged that, despite the best of intentions, Mission 66 was not providing the answers to Yosemite's steadily increasing visitation problems. To those of wilderness persuasion, the always delicate balance between preservation of park wilderness resources and provision for human use had shifted disastrously toward the human end of the spectrum. That many agreed with this point of view was evidenced by the preponderance of articles in the public media that castigated what was being referred to as the "carnival" atmosphere of Yosemite Valley. According to one writer, who had spent three summers as a Park Service ranger in Yosemite,

> It's a fair sized city (40,000 to 60,000 people), complete with smog, crime, juvenile delinquency, parking problems, traffic snarls, rush hours, gang warfare, slums, and urban sprawl. It sprouts every summer in the congested upper end of the spectacularly beautiful Yosemite Valley, heart of Yosemite National Park. This city, despite valiant efforts by the National Park Service to check it, has all but destroyed the atmosphere of peace, wildness, and beauty in this loveliest of valleys. The roar of gigantic waterfalls is drowned out by the roar of motorcycles and hot rods echoing off the cliffs; the deer, plentiful up to ten years ago, have largely moved out to avoid getting heckled by people and their dogs; four thousand campfires morning and evening produce a pall of smoke which, combined with the automobile and stove fumes, hangs in the upper end of the valley making eyes smart and clothes take on a charred odor. The huge garbage removal machines clang great iron trash cans into their mechanical maws with a hideous sound that is easily heard at Glacier Point 3000 feet above. At Fire Fall time (9:30 nightly) there is a two mile traffic jam reminiscent of the commuter rush out of any city—but with more dangerous obsolete roads and traffic patterns. This burgeoning metropolis has changed the center of Yosemite National Park into the Yosemite City Recreation Area, at its worst only slightly less crowded, commercial and honkytonk than Coney Island or Disneyland.[7]

Yosemite Valley was variously described as a "national park nightmare," an "outdoor slum." Crowds of counter-culture young people dressed in "hippy" attire gathered along the banks of the

Merced or kept nearby campers awake through much of the night with their partying, while only yards away, Ahwahnee Hotel guests enjoyed their Yosemite experience in an atmosphere of quiet elegance, much as their forebears had done a century earlier. The Yosemite Village bore a close resemblance to an urban shopping center, but with more congested parking and higher prices. Prostitution and drugs were rampant, particularly in the crowded and noisy campgrounds. Traffic jams seemed interminable, parking at popular scenic points almost impossible. By anyone's definition Yosemite Valley had become a "problem" area.

If Yosemite was considered among the least-wilderness of the national parks, it was also high on the "hit" list of wilderness-minded Park Service leaders who were setting out to return the parks to their primeval state. Even so, most of the changes that began to be implemented in Yosemite were minor and, for the most part, avoided confrontation with the deeply-entrenched and powerful Yosemite Park & Curry Company. Perhaps most noticeable was the controversial discontinuance in 1968 of the famed firefall, bringing the curtain down upon a Yosemite tradition of nearly four-score years. Maintained by director George Hartzog as "artificial" and therefore inconsistent with essential national park values, the firefall had also been the cause of troublesome evening traffic jams in the upper Valley. With the cessation of this attraction it was hoped that some of the congestion might be relieved.

While such an action was something of a tactical victory for the wilderness interests, the fact that more of Yosemite's "artificial" attractions were not acted upon similarly rendered the victory a rather hollow one. In overall terms little was done at first to purge the park of "inappropriate" activities. The removal of the firefall, the dance and movie pavilion, and the unitization of the Valley's campgrounds in order to reduce visitor capacity and uncontrolled camping seemed rather inconsequential in the face of what remained. Critics lashed out at the Valley's golf course, tennis courts, and swimming pools that still smacked of pleasure resort. National parks were not meant to be resorts, it was charged; such developments were "inconsistent with the purposes of the parks."[8]

In their enthusiasm for removing "inconsistent" visitor attractions wilderness advocates even attacked such time-honored outdoor institutions as horseback riding, fishing, and camping. The chief complaints against horses came from hikers and backpackers who objected both to the odor and presence of droppings and the inconvenience of meeting horseback riders on narrow mountain trails. One author recommended that "the number of horses operating for riding in a park must be kept down in the interests of the comfort of pedestrians and in the interest of park visitation."[9] In a study of visitor preference a ranger-naturalist found that "visitors particularly emphasized their dislike for hiking on trails utilized by horses."[10]

With regard to fishing, two highly-influential members of the Conservation Foundation argued that "fishing, surely, is one of those outworn privileges in a national park of the later twentieth century," and one that was now inconsistent with the more important purposes of the national park system. Darling and Eichhorn went on to express similar doubts about the "appropriateness" of camping. "The campground seems to us rather a fetish: it is supposed to recreate for the public the joy of living in the open air, smelling wood smoke and seeing the stars, as so many pioneers were able to do. Putting aside false sentiment, the main attraction of the campground is that it costs so little to the user."[11]

If golf courses, tennis courts, and swimming pools aroused the ire of wilderness purists, there were some forms of outdoor recreation that met with their enthusiastic approval. Probably the most significant of these in terms of numbers involved was backpacking. Facilitated enormously by post-war innovations in camping gear and food preservation techniques, backpackers were mostly young people ranging from their mid-teens to their early thirties who roamed the backcountry in their shorts and "waffle stomper" hiking boots, equipped with the industry's latest technology in light-weight aluminum, nylon, and freeze-dried beef stew. Armed with pocket-sized trail guides and imported cameras, these enthusiasts saw themselves as following in the footsteps of John Muir, "turning almost instinctively to the last remnants of the primeval scene to know again the mystery of the unknown and the beauties of the unchanged terrain." Most backpackers agreed with wilderness poet Sigurd Olson that the national parks had been set aside by their founders principally as temples of primeval nature wherein one could partake of the "universal urge to align himself somehow with those forces and influences" that dominated wild nature throughout the ages.[12] The assumption was, of course, that such "alignment" was most likely to occur on foot and out of sight of such vestiges of civilization as roads, buildings, and, except in moderation, other human beings.

For the most part Yosemite backpackers restricted their activities

Figure 74. Climbers on Lost Arrow, 1984.

to the constructed trails, meadows, and stream-sides, with only occasional forays into really steep or rugged country. In this respect they differed greatly from a relatively new group of outdoors enthusiasts, the mountain or rock climbers. In contrast to backpacking, wherein distances covered and landscapes seen and enjoyed constituted much of the participant's experience, climbing involved a rather more intensive approach to a specific type of landscape. The very steepness and hazards that discouraged conventional backpackers served as a magnet to their more adventuresome counterparts. It should be pointed out that climbing was not new to the Yosemite. Such early explorers as

Clarence King and John Muir had spent considerable time scaling the park's high peaks. Nevertheless, climbing as a popular sport in Yosemite can be said to have originated under the auspices of the Sierra Club, whose members introduced rope climbing from Europe in the early 1930s. As a sport it received additional impetus during World War II as state-of-the-art techniques were employed in the training of mountain troops.

For a decade or so after the war climbing in Yosemite was restricted mostly to the more adventurous members of the Sierra Club. During the 1950s, as the sport became increasingly popular, a new type of climber appeared. Forsaking schools, careers, and marriages in order to practice their "passion," these devotees lived for months in the Valley, often on a hand-to-mouth subsistence basis. In many ways they anticipated and preceded the "drop-out" generation that would follow them in the 1960s, particularly in the way in which their attitudes and life-styles antagonized the "establishment" generations. Whatever their social characteristics, and they were eccentric, to say the least, Yosemite climbers of the late 1950s and 1960s established something of a "golden age" of American climbing. New techniques were developed and old ones perfected, while new climbs of constantly increasing difficulty were conquered on a regular basis. Particularly in the case of "big wall" climbing the Yosemite Valley of the late 1960s "was the most intense climbing scene in North America. The Valley was the place for aspiring American climbers, and big wall climbing was their ideal."[13]

By the late 1960s the popularity of climbing had grown to the extent that the Yosemite Park & Curry Company established its own climbing school, prima facie evidence that climbing had become "legitimized" beyond the social misfit stage. Indeed, proponents of climbing maintained that their sport, more than backpacking or any other kind of outdoor activity, embodied the very essence of rugged wilderness qualities: physical stamina, discipline, athletic ability, courage, supreme powers of concentration, and a sensitivity and willingness to respond to the ultimate of nature's challenges. It did not matter that climbing involved a remarkably small fraction of Yosemite's visitors; by any measure climbing—more specifically big-wall climbing—had achieved a status that placed it on a par with any other visitor activity in the park.

Throughout its history the wilderness movement has instilled within its proponents something of a passion for transcendental primitivism, i.e., the search in nature for experience and/or sensation that transcended the ordinary, that lifted the participant from the common to the sublime. Such a philosophy suggested a certain non-conformity with the conventions and habits of the masses; it also suggested a certain standard of performance and a willingness to meet nature head-on that demanded great stamina and courage. In this context it is easier to understand the sudden popularity and acceptance by the Park Service of cliff-jumping and hang-gliding, two "sports" whose introduction was viewed by many as inconsistent with wilderness era values. The first parachute jumps from El Capitan were made during the 1960s by a pair of jumpers whose round, unsteerable chutes deposited them alive but badly banged up at the bottom of the cliff. The introduction of more sophisticated equipment contributed to both the safety and the popularity of the sport. By 1972 a movie stuntman had employed skis to increase his momentum off the top of El Capitan before deploying his chute, leading to "considerable speculation" about "the possibility of a 'human kite' type event."[14]

The popularity of parachute jumping in Yosemite was abetted by the establishment by Carl Boenish of the BASE system—for Building, Antenna tower, Span (meaning bridges) and Earth (meaning cliffs). Anyone who jumped from all four was entitled to wear a BASE patch. According to Boenish, by the early 1980s forty people had qualified to wear the patch and another two thousand had made at least one qualifying jump. The sport was not without its dangers, to put it mildly; during 1980, the last year that cliff jumping was allowed in Yosemite, twenty-five jumpers were killed. After 1980, despite the Park Service ban, several die-hard jumpers continued to push their luck. During the summer of 1982 a thirty-five-year old parachutist named Jim Tyler was killed while attempting a jump off Half Dome. His two accomplices, afraid of being arrested by park rangers, refused to report the accident, perhaps thereby preventing his rescue. In the furor that followed BASE man Carl Boenish held the National Park Service partly to blame for not allowing the jumpers to "do their thing." "We're doing what we think is right," he asserted, "even if it's against the law. But because it is, we have to take chances we shouldn't have to; we have to always manage to avoid the rangers. How can they expect us to cooperate with them when they want to put us in jail?"[15]

Hang-gliding was another sport that seemed designed specifically for the Yosemite environment. With the aid of a large kite a person could leap off a high cliff and float majestically and relatively safely to

Figure 75. Hang glider.

the ground below. In 1974 the Park Service allowed 170 hang-glider flights from Glacier Point on a "restricted basis." The next year the number of flights had increased to 943; during the following year a total of 1,540 flights was allowed. Although by the early 1980s the number of flights had decreased considerably it was still possible for early-rising visitors to the Valley to see the brightly-colored contraptions wafting their way down from Glacier Point to one of the meadows below, reminiscent, no doubt, of some sort of pre-historic wilderness apparition that somebody thought appropriate in one of the nation's crown jewels.

By the dawn of the 1970s it seemed that the efforts of the wilderness proponents to reform Yosemite had ground to a halt. Visitor habits of long-standing duration, along with a resistance of the concessioners to restrict their marketing activities, created an inertia that appeared to be insurmountable. Thanks to the upcoming master plan fiasco, however, all that was about to change. During the summer of 1974 Yosemite planners, as was customary, submitted a rough draft of the most recent master plan to the park's concessioners for their information and comments. When the final draft, dated August 12, was submitted through Park Service channels for official approval it contained a number of changes that suggested the influence of the park's chief concessioner, the Music Corporation of America. The MCA, as it was generally known, had purchased the Yosemite Park & Curry Company only a year earlier and had already demonstrated its intention of assuming a more active role in Yosemite affairs. When certain proposals in the plan were leaked to the public they immediately came under fire from anti-development minded wilderness advocates who felt provisions in the plan were aimed more toward expanding development within the park rather than reducing or eliminating already existing facilities.

Outcry against the 1974 plan continued to mount until it was officially rejected by the Department of the Interior on the grounds that it favored development interests of the concessioners more than it provided for the preservation of the park's wilderness environments. Yosemite planners were charged with developing a new master plan that not only would be more concerned with preservation but also would guarantee a much greater degree of public participation in the planning process. The program that followed involved the public in a number of ways, from the distribution of rather detailed questionnaires regarding planning options to the holding of public hearings in selected cities across the nation. Although the participants in this process could scarcely be considered as representative of either the American or the Yosemite visitor population, the results underscored the tremendous diversity of opinion regarding the "true" purposes of national parks. They also suggested the degree of emotional attachment that many Americans felt toward "their" parks. Participant responses were offered with fervor and conviction; seldom was there inclination toward compromise or middle ground position. Many who attended and spoke at the hearings were upper-class and highly educated citizens of California and most of them were considerably parochial in their views. Despite the wide range of opinions expressed at the hearings, however, there was general agreement that the park, particularly the Valley, was overdeveloped and that more attention needed to be given to the preservation of the park's wilderness values.

After nearly six years of expensive and extensive effort the General Management Plan of 1980 was finally approved as the official planning document for Yosemite National Park. In general it was a reasonable reflection of how public opinion—at least the more vocal elements thereof—had come to perceive the Yosemite landscape. Basic to its philosophy was the assumption that the principal intent of the national parks movement was the preservation, where possible, and the restoration, where necessary, of America's wilderness heritage. Inherent to this philosophy was the clear understanding that human utilization of national park landscapes should be minimal and only on "nature's" terms. In essence the plan called for a return to a more "natural" and undeveloped Yosemite landscape. Of particular significance was the plan to remove from the Valley all developments and facilities but those absolutely necessary for the protection of visitors and park resources. Most of these facilities, particularly those of the Park Service, were to be relocated down the narrow Merced River Canyon to El Portal, just outside the park boundaries. Another significant objective was the ultimate ban of private automobiles in Yosemite Valley. Various forms of mass transit were envisioned that would provide visitors with a peaceful, non-polluting, and carefully managed wilderness experience. Developments reflecting traditional Yosemite visitor experiences that were no longer considered appropriate, such as golf courses, tennis courts, and beauty parlors, were to be discontinued, while improved interpretation efforts were planned to ensure "that a visit to Yosemite (would become) a lifetime treasure."

In many ways the 1980 plan was but another in a long series of efforts to scale down development in the Valley. According to former director Conrad Wirth, the 1949 master plan for Yosemite National Park had proposed the development of the Big Meadows area, outside but overlooking the Yosemite Valley, for visitor accommodations. It was hoped that this would gradually phase out the overcrowding of overnight facilities in the valley. The proposal was based on the intent of reducing the visitor impact by gradually establishing day use for a major portion of the valley.[16] It will be remembered that one of the objectives of Mission 66 had been the "removal of all but absolutely necessary operating facilities from the valley." Most of these facilities were to be relocated to El Portal, thereby freeing "more of the precious and scarce Valley floor for visitor use and enjoyment."[17]

Visitor accommodations and Park Service support facilities were not the only developments that park planners planned to reduce in the Valley. For decades the most congested, noisy, and environmentally abused of the Valley's landscapes had been the public campgrounds. Initially, people who chose to camp in Yosemite were simply directed by park rangers to those areas designated for public camping. Located mostly in the upper Valley along both sides of the Merced River these areas had no individually designated campsites as such; rather, as long as one could squeeze one's camp outfit into a space somewhere they were legally entitled to do so. This practice resulted in numerous problems, particularly on crowded holiday weekends. On such occasions it was not uncommon for one camper to awaken in the morning and find that during the night another camper had moved in and set up his tent in the middle of the first camper's campsite, often "sharing" his tent stakes and support ropes. It was commonly joked—and not without some truth—that the first camper to drive his automobile out of the campground on a holiday morning was likely to dismantle half the campground in the process due to the common practice of securing tent lines to the handiest object available—including automobile bumpers.

Particularly aggravating to park rangers was the widespread tendency of campers to disregard the roads into camping areas. When it was not convenient, or when the campgrounds seemed full, visitors often drove their automobiles directly across the meadows or wherever else their inclinations suggested. A rather simple but practical solution to this problem had involved the construction of "moral ditches" along the sides of roads which, according to Ranger Garrison, "not only prevented evening roadside parking by youthful lovers (but) also channeled driving and protected the forest floor from wandering motorists."[18]

Over the years the Park Service had taken various steps to deal with the crowds and squalor of what were becoming known as the "canvas jungles." The first, begun in the inter-war era, reduced the amount of time that a camper could spend in a campground, from an unlimited time to thirty days, then to several weeks. In the long run, however, the most practicable solution was the "unitization" of the campgrounds, i.e., the establishment of individual campsites in camping areas. When a campground's allotted sites were occupied the campground was considered full and closed to additional campers. Unitization began in the 1940s and was pretty much concluded by the latter 1960s. At the

Figure 76. Camping out-of-bounds, Camp 14, 1951.

same time the campgrounds were being unitized the actual number of campsites in the Valley was reduced and a ban placed on all overflow camping. Subsequent efforts to deal with overcrowded campground conditions resulted in seven-day use limits and a reservation system that finally dispensed with the long lines of hopeful but likely to be disappointed campers that had gathered at campground entrances every summer morning for decades.

Adding to the overcrowding problem in park campgrounds was the increasing popularity of recreation vehicles. Since the days of the touring car national park visitors had demonstrated a remarkable proclivity for vehicles designed especially for travel. Until the 1930s, when they began to be commercially manufactured, the ancestors of today's recreation vehicles (RVs) were hand-made contraptions that reflected both the artistic genius and mechanical ingenuity of their builders. About a decade or so after World War II, the production of RVs leaped into full gear and Yosemite campgrounds were soon frequented by increasing numbers of tent trailers, aluminum travel trailers, and self-contained motor homes. By the early 1970s 10 percent of Yosemite's campers were using RVs; a decade later more than half as many campers came in RVs (339,074) as came with tents (665,191). From the perspective of campground managers the onslaught of the ever-larger RVs presented special problems: RV owners wanted utility hook-ups and waste drainage facilities and larger parking spaces than traditional tent campers, while the latter often objected to the transformation of their woodsy campsite into just another suburban mobile home park. The attempted solution was one of segregation; certain campgrounds were designated as tent-only areas while others permitted camping vehicles and were better equipped to service their particular needs.

Of all the attempts to deal with Yosemite Valley's crowds and confusion the most effective were those that dealt with traffic control. By the latter 1960s vehicular traffic on the Valley's narrow roads had become a problem of crisis proportions. Long lines of stop and go traffic frayed nerves and upset carefully worked out itineraries. Lack of parking spaces produced massive jams near stores, visitor centers, and scenic pull-outs. Frustrated tourists often quite literally "took to the woods" with their problem, parking their automobiles, pickup campers, and even giant mobile homes wherever they could find a space between trees, rocks, etc. The result was esthetically disturbing and environmentally disastrous. For many tourists the logistics of travel in the Valley were so aggravating that their entire Yosemite experience was adversely affected.

With considerable trepidation park managers finally decided to take the bull by the horns, so to speak, and confront the issue of separating the American tourists from their beloved automobiles. The

Figure 77. An early recreational vehicle.

results were immediate and surprisingly satisfactory. Such inaccessible and traditionally congested areas as the Mariposa Grove of Giant Sequoia and the roads to Mirror Lake and Happy Isles were closed to all private vehicles. All parking was banned from the Yosemite Village plaza in front of the Valley visitor center and the area turned into a visitor mall, "reserved for concerts, ranger-naturalist programs, bicycling, and a visitor promenade." "But the best moves we made," said Superintendent Lynn Thompson, "were the establishment of free bus systems and making the valley road pattern into a one-way loop."[19] In a major break with tradition the Park Service purchased a number of tram-like buses to be used by visitors at no charge. After several years of experimenting with schedules and vehicles a remarkably efficient system of mass transportation evolved. Currently a fleet of diesel-powered buses makes continuous loops around the upper Valley, stopping at fixed destinations every ten minutes or so during the summer months. The service is free to all visitors and allows them to circulate about the upper Valley freely and with none of the problems incidental to the use of private vehicles. Particularly in the east end of the Valley and near the Mall the buses are the only vehicles allowed on the roads, a welcome change from the congested conditions of earlier days. The rest of the Valley road system has been turned largely into a one-way pattern, a result of which has been an enormous improvement in roadside pull-out opportunities for those who want to pause momentarily at a particularly scenic point.

With minor exceptions the traffic control measures have met with widespread approval from park managers and public alike. Shortly into the new program, in 1971 the shuttle buses carried more than 1.6 million passengers. Just several years earlier, claimed an elated Director George Hartzog, "to carry that many people would have required 400,000 car trips." Several years later surveys indicated that eighty-five percent of those riding the shuttles were favorably disposed toward them. Noted Yosemite personality Ansel Adams was quoted as saying "I have never seen Yosemite looking so well and people happier in it." He credited the shuttle system with having much to do with this turn of events, referring to it as "a newly evolving appropriate human participation and enjoyment of this park."[20]

Negative comments about the shuttles usually revolved around their odor and their noise and the fact that certain people, particularly young people and "senior citizens," were in the habit of "joyriding" for hours on the buses. It was true that at times the upper Valley sounded much like a training school for diesel truck drivers; however, one could hardly fault people for utilizing the buses for joyriding. After all, prior to the shuttle system the same individuals might very well have done the same thing but in their own automobiles. Moreover, one surely must be understanding toward someone who feels the scenic magnificence of Yosemite Valley warrants more than one sightseeing loop around the bus line. This is particularly so in the case of elderly or infirm persons who are uncomfortable with bus steps and path conditions—no matter how well groomed.

As far as park management was concerned the explosion in backpacking popularity that accompanied the wilderness movement presented serious challenges in Yosemite's High Sierra. Beginning in the 1960s the number of people entering the "backcountry" began to increase rapidly. By the peak year of 1975 nearly 79,000 visitors spent approximately 219,000 nights in Yosemite's undeveloped "wilderness." Use decreased somewhat in the following decade to an average of 60,260 people spending about 165,000 visitor nights per year. The majority of backcountry users were young white males from some part of California; one-fifth of them were in the Yosemite backcountry for the first time. Regardless of their sex or origins most of these backpackers were considerably more enthusiastic than skilled and were seldom ecologically sophisticated enough to understand the environmental ramifications of their actions. Favorite campsites became heavily abused, trees scarred or cut down in the endless search for firewood, fire rings proliferated, stream and lakesides spotted with soap and toothpaste residue, scraps of toilet paper sprouted like mushrooms behind logs and rocks, paths proliferated endlessly across and around meadowlands, while litter accumulated from one end of the High Sierra to another at a rate that would have caused John Muir to choke on his sierra cup.

The Park Service's answer to this problem was the formation in 1973 of the Yosemite backcountry management team. Over the next several years a plan evolved that divided the backcountry into use zones. Quotas were then established for each zone and permits issued for entry points or trailheads. When the number of permits issued for a particular trailhead reached the maximum allowed by the quota visitors were required to either choose a different area or postpone their trip. As part of the process of applying for a permit the prospective backcountry user was made aware of a variety of regulations designed to protect not only the ecologically fragile backcountry environment

Figure 78. Contemporary shuttle bus.

but also the rights of other users. Seasonal rangers traversed the backcountry on a regular basis checking on permit compliance and generally taking a low-key, friendly approach toward non-conformers. Happily both the system and the personable approach taken by Park Service personnel seem to have succeeded, even though the resulting "wilderness" experience might not provide quite the "outstanding opportunity for solitude and/or primitive and unconfined type of recreation" that the user envisioned for himself.

Without question the past three decades have wrought momentous changes in how Americans have perceived and utilized the Yosemite landscape. During the years immediately following World War II the dominant mode of use can best be described as a continuation of the Mather era philosophy of parks as national vacation areas. With the tremendous surge in visitation rates that followed the war, however, it became painfully apparent that a policy of developing park resources to meet ever-increasing visitor demands did not serve the long-range best interests of either the park or the visitors. In part a reaction against what was perceived as over-development, the wilderness movement of the 1960s and 1970s persistently and adamantly maintained that the most appropriate mission of the Yosemite National Park was the preservation of its wilderness and that all management efforts should be directed toward that goal. Facilitated by the pressure tactics of environmental activism the wilderness movement came to exert a tremendous influence upon the perception and use of Yosemite. As discussed earlier this influence had been present in the park for some time but was probably felt most keenly during the 1974 master plan controversy. With the appearance of the 1980 plan the official policy became the reduction or removal from the park of those activities and facilities not in harmony with the restoration of Yosemite to near-wilderness conditions. The clearly stated intent was to re-shape the traditionally diverse visitor experience in such a way that the principal components thereof would become the appreciation and preservation of wilderness.

In any attempt to describe the evolving Yosemite visitor experience it must be acknowledged that the ways in which Americans have perceived and utilized the Yosemite are extremely diverse. As might be expected, this diversity only increased over the years as each new generation of visitors introduced its own particular biases and behaviors. For the most part such changes in visitor fashions merely added to—rather than replaced—existing ones with the result that the contemporary Yosemite visitor experience is at least as diverse as the almost three million people who frequent the park each year. Even so, a number of important generalizations can be made about the influence of the wilderness movement upon the perception and use patterns of contemporary Yosemite visitors. These changes included an increasing popularity of certain types of visitor activities, especially backpacking and climbing, the reduction and reorganization of overnight accommodation facilities, and a revolution of sorts in transportation patterns, mainly in the Valley.

More importantly, perhaps, there has occurred a fundamental shift in attitude that has affected National Park Service personnel as well as visitors. (Concessioner attitude toward wilderness, quite understandably, has been somewhat less than enthusiastic.) Traditional modes of park enjoyment, from guided bus tours to dining at the Ahwahnee, not only have fallen somewhat out of fashion but are often considered suspect by those immersed in what Alston Chase refers to as "primitive chic." To most wilderness advocates any type of activity or attitude that does not directly enhance one's experience with Yosemite's wilderness is considered of questionable value, at best, and possibly inappropriate or even threatening. Viewed as particularly onerous in this regard is the insistence of many visitors to experience the wilderness from within the confines of their automobiles. Decried as the single greatest evil within today's national parks, the automobile has come a long way from the day when Mather and his contemporaries proclaimed its virtues as both an exciting new form of recreation and a great expediter of national travel.

Perhaps more subtle than the changes in visitor activities were the shifts that occurred in interpretation efforts. Prior to the wilderness era the principal intent of park naturalists was to facilitate visitors' understanding and enjoyment of nature by introducing them to a friendly world of plants, animals, and natural processes. Ever implicit was the possibility that human beings and wild creatures were basically compatible, if man were only willing, and therefore quite capable of developing some sort of mutually beneficial relationship. All this changed during the environmentally activist decades of the 1960s and 1970s. As discussed earlier one of the underlying philosophies of the wilderness movement was the contention that man was an alien to wilderness. As such his behavior and artifacts—even his very presence—represented a potential threat to the integrity and well-being of wild nature.

Park Service naturalists were gradually indoctrinated in the "new" ecology and with the proselyting zeal characteristic of the times set out to convert the traveling public to their way of thinking. While much of what followed was laudatory from a scientific viewpoint, the approach taken sometimes reflected more the dogmatic activism of the 1960s than a sophisticated understanding of ecological processes. In short, the change in philosophy was not without its problems. Many an old-time park visitor was both nonplussed and a bit angered by his change in status; rather than being welcomed to the park by the genial gentlemen in green he suddenly found himself treated with condescension as an unschooled, rather bungling persona non grata whose presence in the wilderness was an intrusion and possibly even a threat. This suggestion of an adversarial relationship between man and nature found expression in several ways, from the attempt to remove visitors from all contact with wildlife (usually by employing "scare" tactics— "this animal is dangerous! Do not approach it!"), to the constant inference that human interaction with the natural world is inevitably detrimental.

Equally disturbing was the frequently-voiced contention that the preservation of wilderness areas like the Yosemite held the key to the future well-being of our planet. Contemporary park visitors have become a little too sophisticated to accept such simplistic solutions to complex problems. On a strictly scientific basis it is difficult to understand how the ecological processes operative in remote mountain environments offer solutions to the problem of maintaining productivity in those ecosystems in which the majority of the world's population lives. Moreover, at a time when nuclear weapons are proliferating among nations known less for their social conscience than for their militant self-interest it is felt by many that "in wilderness is not necessarily the preservation of the world."

In assuming more of an activist role in environmental education the Park Service introduced a number of programs that proved popular with the public. "How-to" sessions on backpacking and nature photography joined traditional nature hikes and campfire programs as naturalists sought to educate visitors as well as facilitate their enjoyment of the park. Evening concerts of a rather more formal nature featured a variety of offerings, from a highly nostalgic rendering of a John Muir dialogue to a spectacular film presentation on Yosemite big wall climbing. Especially popular with young people were the "ecology float trips" on the Merced River. Led by a ranger/naturalist in a rubber raft the guided float trips were offered at no cost to anyone who could muster and ride a floatable device down a mile or so of the river. Especially satisfying to many visitors was the expanded Indian exhibit in the vicinity of the Mall. Staffed largely by Indian employees, the exhibit attempted to portray native life in Yosemite Valley during the 1870-1880 period. Liberal use of "hands-on" techniques and personal conversation between visitors and "residents" of the reconstructed village provided visitors with an experience that was as entertaining as it was educational.

A rather recent challenge to interpretive programs has been the increase of visitors from different ethnic and/or cultural backgrounds. By the early 1980s approximately 30 percent of the park's visitors fell into this category. Approximately 275,000 of these were classified as non-English speaking. A language barrier of this magnitude posed serious and immediate challenges for park management personnel, both in the Park Service and in the Yosemite Park & Curry Company. The biggest challenge was faced by the Park Service, whose communication needs were considerably more complex and abstract than those of the concessioner. It was considerably easier, for example, to help a foreign tourist with a menu selection than it was to bring him or her to an understanding of the values associated with wilderness preservation and the role of the national park system as it pertained thereto. In those cases where Spanish was the foreign language involved, it was possible for some park employees raised in California to muddle through an explanation of something with at least some hope of getting through to the visitor. With the increasing numbers of East Asians visiting Yosemite, however, the problem was rather more serious. At present the National Park Service is attempting to deal with the problem not only by hiring specialists in foreign languages but also by preparing interpretive presentations designed with the values and mores of specific cultures in mind.

By the middle 1980s it was apparent that the wilderness movement had brought many changes to the ways that visitors viewed and enjoyed Yosemite. While some of these changes were a function of the official redefinition of the purpose of national parks, others reflected the changing attitudes of individual park managers and interpreters. As far as the visitor experience was concerned most of these changes tended to restrict the options available for visitor use of park resources. While many visitors sympathized with the need for such changes, others felt an increasing sense of dissatisfaction at policies which were often perceived as discriminatory and arbitrary. This dissatisfaction was compounded by the attitudes of some park personnel. Unlike the generally upbeat "what-can-I-do-to-help-you-enjoy-your-park-visit" mentality that characterized former times, today's Park Service employee sometimes conveys the impression that he/she is there to protect the park from the visitor, who is suspected of harboring intentions of degrading the primeval wilderness or otherwise engaging in "inappropriate" activities.

In their attempt to restrict visitor activities to those appropriate to a wilderness setting park managers were sometimes accused of favoring a rather small and elite element of the traveling public. It was difficult for many visitors to understand why it was necessary for them to leave their automobiles and walk to a scenic point in order to appreciate it, or why it was inappropriate to sleep in a bed and eat meals that were prepared and served under a roof by professional hoteliers. They resented the implication that they were second class citizens and a threat to the national park landscape if they did not choose to or were unable to "rough it" in the manner prescribed by contemporary wilderness purists. Aggravating this sense of insult were the inconsistencies displayed by Park Service officials in their determination of what kinds of activities were appropriate in the park. Just exactly how congruent to the wilderness ideal were hang-gliders and yellow rubber rafts?

Despite these complaints (and it should be noted that visitors to the Yosemite have always complained about something), visitation to the park shows no signs of diminishing. In fact, according to the director of the Yosemite Research Center, Jan W. van Wagtendonk, summer visitation has consistently reached the overnight capacity of the park's campgrounds and accommodations since the latter 1960s. In his study of visitor use patterns in Yosemite, van Wagtendonk pointed out that increases in use could only occur by additional visitation during the off-peak months from September through May, by increased use of the backcountry, by a reduction in the number of nights a party stays in the park, thereby increasing turnover, or by an increase in day users.[21] It is both a testimony to Yosemite's attractiveness and a symptom of the park's greatest problem that each of these increases has occurred in recent years.

What is more impressive is the way that the National Park Service has dealt with these increases. Visitor grumblings notwithstanding, the Yosemite of the latter 1980s was a vastly different place than it was a mere twenty years earlier. Most noticeable, perhaps, was a tremendous reduction in the congestion that characterized Yosemite Valley during the 1960s. While by no means as serenely wild as it was when James Hutchings led his first tourist party there over a century ago, it nevertheless was vastly more quiet and peaceful than it had been for decades. The flow of visitor traffic—both on and off the roads—was handled remarkably well. The campgrounds were quieter and campsites more spacious. The presence of the concessioner was less obtrusive, while the one-time carnival atmosphere of Camp Curry had been greatly reduced. Gone was the Ahwahnee golf course with its barbed wire-topped chain link fence (the Camp Curry swimming pool still remained). Gone also was the horribly crowded parking area that used to front the museum and Valley Visitor Center. In its place was a reasonably peaceful if overly-paved expanse of asphalt on which visitors could be seen eating, relaxing, or participating in an interpretive activity. Nearby were the superbly done Indian village exhibit and the less-superbly done restaurants, gift, and camera supplies shops. The interpretive offerings of the Park Service, regardless of their philosophical bent, were varied and generally well-done. (The fact that these programs changed from time to time was necessary if the large percentage of Yosemite visitors who were repeaters was to be attracted to them.)

Outside the Valley the changes of the last twenty years were also generally commendable, if less apparent. Despite the popularity of the High Sierra for backpacking, the quality of the backcountry experience was maintained at a high level. The pioneer village at Wawona had become an effective vehicle for helping visitors develop a feel for Yosemite's pioneer past. The tranquility and majesty of the Mariposa Grove had been considerably enhanced by the removal of automobiles from its narrow roads. And while the golf course and tennis courts remained near the Wawona Hotel complex they seemed less incongruous there than in the heart of Yosemite Valley. Throughout the entire park the visitor experience reflected the thoughtful planning, careful management, and generally courteous touch of the National Park Service. And while it was probably impossible for visitors and management to ever reach agreement on what constituted "appropriate" use of the park resources, the kinds of visitor activities that were blatantly at variance with Yosemite's wilderness or scenic heritage were largely absent. (Sightings of brightly-colored, pterodactyl-like creatures could still be made of a morning in the vicinity of Glacier Point.) All of the above is not to say that Yosemite management had solved its many problems. The difficulties of juggling crowds of people, delicate ecosystems, and the ever-present pressures of special interest groups posed formidable challenges to Yosemite's keepers—National Park Service, concessioners, and public alike. But the fact that troublesome problems remained to be solved—the drug situation, for example—should never obfuscate or detract from the fact that truly remarkable accomplishments had occurred and that, in the main, the impact of the wilderness era upon the Yosemite had been both substantial and positive.

Chapter 7
Epilogue

AT THE TIME THAT YOSEMITE and other early national parks were established it would have been difficult to envision a day when too much visitor use would become the park's greatest management challenge. Depending upon one's definition of preservation that day was reached either well before or shortly after World War II. In Yosemite, as well as in other national parks, the relationship between preservation and use has been complicated by changing perceptions and habits. At the same time that use pressures were mounting in both intensity and variety the definition of what constituted appropriate preservation became increasingly restrictive. Over the years a gradual and, perhaps, inevitable reinterpretation of the national parks enabling legislation has taken place. Whereas the founders of the parks clearly intended that these outstanding repositories of natural/historic scenery be preserved for the use and enjoyment of the American people, today's Park Service policy makers have redefined them as "vignettes of pristine America" to be preserved and valued primarily as wilderness.

In Yosemite the changes wrought by the wilderness movement have been both substantial and controversial but have gone a long way toward solving the park's most pressing problems. The question now becomes a matter of how far the Park Service should go in restoring the Yosemite to "wilderness" conditions. There are those who have served notice that they will not rest until all overnight accommodations, gift shops, gasoline stations, and employee residences are removed from Yosemite Valley. There are others, particularly those involved with the above developments, that are equally determined to stay. In both cases compelling arguments can be made to support their point of view. What is the answer? Probably no one knows, but since a book of this type would be incomplete without some kind of recommendation for future action the following suggestions are offered in the hope that Yosemite's second century as a national park will be at least as satisfactory as its first.

A fundamental tenet of the wilderness movement has been that wilderness should be valued for biocentric (non-human) rather than anthropocentric (human) reasons. Those who advocate biocentrism suggest that the rights of wild communities should be both acknowledged and respected and that when human beings enter those communities they should do so only on "nature's terms." While this notion has a certain emotional appeal it is not based upon scientific fact. If we accept the premise of science that the earth and its processes are apersonal—that is, neither planned nor influenced by any intentional directive or force (such as God)—we must conclude that any "rights" accorded ecosystems and their plant and/or animal components—including humans—are purely of human invention. Simply put, except in context of human culture, nature has no "terms" except for those we as human beings assign it. The fact that wilderness advocates continue to intervene in what they feel is a defense of the "rights" of an endangered species, for example, is but another expression—no matter how well intended—of a peculiarly human conceit. Wilderness itself is a condition of nature definable as such only by humans. This is as much the case in national parks as in any other of earth's environments.

From their very beginnings national parks have been anthropocentric in definition. After all, it was people who assigned particular value to places like Yosemite and Yellowstone and agitated for their special status. National parks are clearly and simply the invention of human beings. Let us value and treat them as the cultural institutions that they are, defined first and still most definitively by the enabling legislation that gave them birth. The national park idea, i.e., the preservation of extraordinary examples of a nation's heritage for the enjoyment of future generations, is at once one of the most idealistic and innovative creations of the American civilization. "Parks are for the understanding of nature and ourselves; they are for the inspiration which comes from lonely commune with nature and the forces which shape our environment; they are for solace for those troubled by the turbulence of modern civilization." The eloquence of former lifetime ranger Lon Garrison is not cheapened in the slightest by the recognition that the above description of national park purposes is meaningful only within the context of culture. As he knew only too well there were people within his own society who could spend days in Yosemite or Yellowstone and still emerge "unscathed" from an exposure to the most impressive of our national parks.

Garrison went on to suggest that one of the most important purposes of our national parks was to "invoke patriotism and develop pride in our homeland and all that it has to offer."[1] In a very real sense the national parks are an important expression of what the American civilization has perceived as esthetically noteworthy in the natural landscape. They represent the epitome of what we as a people have defined as scenic beauty and, at the same time, are an expression of the rather peculiar form of altruism that is characteristic of our democratic approach to civilization. Their roots, like those of most of our culture, are traceable to our European origins and yet it was in the context of our infant republic's search for an esthetic identity that they came to life. The legacy of our national parks and our perceptions thereof are a manifestation of an American interpretation of nature, the visual expression of which has included the works of such landscape artists as Thomas Cole and Albert Bierstadt. As such they should be both revered and maintained as treasure troves of our national culture. The fact that they are yet imperfect specimens of wilderness in no way lessens their historic worth. After all, national parks were established more as outdoor museums than as wilderness preserves. In fact, it can be argued that their museum value is likely to be the most durable in the long run. For the most part the scenic attractions of the national parks can be enjoyed— indeed, they have been enjoyed for many decades—under less than true wilderness conditions. It can even be argued that most of those who visit and enjoy the parks are unable to distinguish between wilderness and near-substitutes anyway. Given the fact that wilderness is mainly a state of mind and minds tend to change frequently, it seems likely that the singularity and the sheer dimensions of an El Capitan, Half Dome, or Yosemite Falls will be of more lasting appeal than their wilderness qualities.

Let us return to the notion that our national parks were established as parks to be seen and enjoyed by the American people. Let us encourage visitors to understand and appreciate the uniqueness of the features they were established to preserve. And at the same time let us give credit to the National Park Service for successfully walking the fine line between visitor use and environmental preservation. At a time when it is immensely more popular to criticize than commend it is almost heresy to suggest that in carrying out its manifold responsibilities the Park Service has done a decent, perhaps even admirable job, and yet it is my opinion that this is the case. Nevertheless, there is room for concern that the Service might be neglecting its responsibility to manage the parks for *all* Americans. Particularly in its zeal to

Figure 79. Yosemite Visitors Center.

implement wilderness philosophy the Park Service must never forget that use of the parks by the American people is still "the best means by which (their) basic purpose is realized and is the best guarantee of perpetuating the System."[2] In all its deliberations the Service would be well advised to remember the fact that it is the average American citizen, viz a viz the political arena, who is the "owner, the banker, and the principal user of the National Park System."[3]

In this respect it is of great importance that the Park Service remain sensitive to the needs of those visitors who are, as yet, unconverted to the value of wilderness. Altogether too often wilderness advocates demonstrate a remarkable insensitivity to the interests of others in their assumption that theirs is the only "truly" appropriate perception and use of the national parks. This attitude is manifest in many ways but most objectionable, perhaps, by the tendency to belittle, disparage, or otherwise "make fun of" the "average" park tourist. Despite the fact that there are millions of them and that they comprise the majority of visitors in every park, the implication is plain that as a group they have not caught the vision of what national parks represent in our society. Just what constitutes an "average" tourist is difficult to say, but in Yosemite, at least, there seems to be a certain amount of agreement about what such a creature is not. The average tourist is apparently not a true devotee of wilderness; he/she does not habitually frequent the remote backcountry portions of the park and is not an outspoken advocate of removing all visitor accommodations and automobiles from the Valley. Rather, "average" tourists seem more inclined to spend most of their time in those areas that are accessible to their automobiles. They generally choose to patronize the concessioner-operated lodging facilities or the drive-in campgrounds. They usually come as families but often are part of a tour group. Seldom can such tourists be described as young, vigorous, and adventurous; rather, if we are to believe the insinuations of waitresses, backpackers, and even the occasional park ranger, average tourists are usually over-weight, poor-ly-mannered, physically unfit, and esthetically insensitive proletarians who as often as not drive a gas-guzzling station wagon filled to the windows with noisy youngsters whose chief concerns are the locations of the nearest comfort stations and soft drink dispensing machines. As one park employee put it, the typical visitor is "the person who comes in a car, buys a hot dog, looks at the waterfalls and big rocks, then leaves."4 Among those tourists who do not consider themselves as typical or average there is a generally shared conviction that the latter are hampered by perceptual deficiencies that commonly—if inadver-tently—render them incapable of appreciating the park's finer values. A more extremist view suggests that their presence in the park is a desecration of the very wilderness that the park is there to preserve.

It would appear that the National Park Service in Yosemite, in its emphasis on wilderness, shares the conviction that the "average" tourist should play a diminishing role in the park. Repeated throughout the general management plan is the goal of getting visitors away from their automobiles, their hotel/motel beds and dining rooms, and other-wise modifying their Yosemite visit so as to produce a more "ap-propriate" wilderness experience. Ever present is the implication that a wilderness experience represents not only the highest mode of park perception but perhaps the only one that is ultimately acceptable. This type of attitude tempts both concessioner and Park Service employees to belittle the tourist who spends the bulk of his/her Yosemite time viewing the traditional attractions of the Valley. Visitors are con-tinuously urged to get out of the confines of the Valley and experience the "true" Yosemite of the High Sierra. This attitude, by the way, has been expressed repeatedly since the great outdoors era of the late nineteenth and early twentieth centuries. As we have seen it was virtually gospel among the ranks of the Sierra Club that the only "real" Yosemite experience was to be found in the High Sierra.

Contemporary rangers fall into a similar trap when they suggest to park visitors that if they want to experience the "true" Yosemite they must leave the crowds and confusion of the Valley for the tranquility and pristine beauty of the backcountry wilderness. Such a recommendation implies that because the Valley can no longer be considered as wilderness, its cliffs, waterfalls, and meadows have somehow suffered as scenic attractions, and that visitors who choose to restrict their sightseeing to the Valley are somehow the recipients of an inferior visitor experience. Such an attitude would have been astonishing to the likes of James Hutchings or Galen Clark. As a matter of fact, such an attitude would be astonishing to many who come to today's Yosemite and find themselves caught up by the extraordinary scenery of an admittedly "unwilderness" Yosemite Valley. In defense of the "average" tourist it must be reiterated that perception and appreciation of nature are subjective and intensely personal phenomena. It is not only intellectually untenable but foolish to suggest that some tourists are inferior to others because they perceive and value different components of the scenic landscape. It would also seem both unwise and impolitic for the National Park Service to be favoritist in its attitudes toward certain types of visitors. No matter how unsophisticated or non-disposed toward wilderness they might be, "average" visitors not only have equal rights to visit the Yosemite but are equally represented in Congress, a fact that a politically vulnerable National Park Service might be well advised to remember.

Particularly during the past decade or so the National Park Service has come under repeated and harsh criticism for its failure to restructure the parks as strictly wilderness areas. In their single-minded zeal to promote their cause such critics exhibit little empathy for the Park Service's attempts to resolve its chronic legislative dilemma. Required by law to both protect park resources and provide for their use by visitors, the Service finds itself continuously frustrated by the need to foster simultaneously two basically incompatible efforts. That they should experience difficulty with this dilemma should hardly be surprising. As pointed out by Dorothy Bradley, a member of the Montana House of Representatives, the impossible charge given the National Park Service seemed to be based on the "largely unsupported conviction that there are extraordinary qualities in ordinary people."[5] Unfortunately for the Park Service (and the rest of the world), the supply of people "extraordinary" enough to find an amicable solution to the national parks dilemma is extraordinarily meager, to say the least.

Aside from the fact that nothing the Park Service can do will please everybody—or, perhaps, even a majority—there are never enough resources available to accomplish even the goals that it has established for itself. The chronic underfunding that plagued the Yosemite Valley Commission more than a century ago is still very much a fact of everyday life. Were a member of that commission to be reincarnated as a contemporary Yosemite ranger he would feel right at home in being given a one dollar budget to accomplish a five dollar job. No one said it any better than John Ise when he pointed out that the difference between some of the Park Service administrators and the purists who have scolded them for too much development, for "departing from true park standards," is to some extent the difference between men who have a practical job to do and those of "fine idealism who do not have these responsibilities."[6] This certainly is not to say that the Park Service has not made mistakes or catered to special interests in ways that have not been in the best interests of the parks.

But what are the "best interests" of the parks? Most people who have anything to do with them are quite certain that they have the correct answers; unfortunately they seldom agree with each other and often disagree strongly with the mandates that are given the Park Service by Congress. When one considers the gap between the enormous challenges and the chronically insufficient resources allocated to the agency one can't help but be amazed at how well they do. No matter what the basis for evaluation the National Park Service is comprised largely of underpaid, overworked, highly motivated, idealistic, and dedicated individuals. That they should be so widely unappreciated is not only unfair but also an embarrassment to all who are interested in national park matters. Furthermore, given the complexity of demands placed upon Park Service officials by special interest groups, their traditional policy of "making haste slowly" seems more than reasonable. In following what some have described as a "middle-of-the-road" policy, the Service has demonstrated repeatedly its awareness of its original mandate, that the national parks were to be preserved for all Americans to see and enjoy.

In the final analysis the national park idea is much like our laws or our national constitution: both are based upon cultural premises and therefore are totally arbitrary. As such they are vulnerable to changes in interpretation and difficult to justify on purely scientific grounds. During the coming years it is inevitable that the parks, like the laws that help define how we perceive ourselves as a society, will undergo change as their managers attempt to deal with new interpretations and the challenges they represent. Whatever it is that the Park Service needs

Figure 80. Children at Yosemite Falls.

to do to meet those challenges, I am in full agreement with Horace Albright's fervent plea on behalf of what he considered to be his favorite park, Yosemite. "I hope no new policy will discourage visitors who really want to see this exquisite part of our native landscape."[7] With any luck at all our national parks will continue indefinitely to inspire the American people much as the Yosemite Valley did the great showman Phineas T. Barnum. "Unsurpassed and unsurpassable," he wrote in 1870. "Look around with pleasure and upward with gratitude."

Notes

Chapter 1   *Introduction*

1. Act of August 25, 1916 (39 Stat. L., 535)—An Act To establish a National Park Service and for other purposes (as amended by act of June 2, 1920: 41 Stat. L., 732—An Act To Accept the cession by the State of California of exclusive jurisdiction of the lands embraced within the Yosemite National Park, Sequoia National Park, and General Grant National Park, respectively and for other purposes).

Chapter 2   *The Discovery of the "Yo Semite"*

1. Thomas Starr King, *A Vacation Among The Sierras: Yosemite in 1860*, edited with introduction and notes by John A. Hussey (San Francisco: The Book Club of California, 1962), 43–49.

2. *The Country Gentleman* (Albany, October 8, 1856), 243.

3. *Illustrated Handbook of American Travel* (New York: 1857), 377. Later known as *Appleton's Handbook*.

4. Horace Greeley, *An Overland Journey from New York to San Francisco in the Summer of 1859* (New York: 1860), 309.

5. Samuel Bowles, *Across the Continent* (Springfield: Samuel Bowles & Company; New York: Hurd & Houghton, 1865), viii, 224.

6. Edward Halsey Foster, *The Civilized Wilderness: Backgrounds to American Romantic Literature, 1817-1860* (New York and London: The Free Press, 1975), 13.

7. Roland Van Zandt, *The Catskill Mountain House* (New Brunswick: Rutgers University Press, 1966), 157.

8. Stella Margetson, *Leisure and Pleasure in the Nineteenth Century* (New York: Coward-Mc-Cann, Inc., 1969), 84.

9. V. S. Naipaul, *An Area of Darkness* (New York: Macmillan, 1964), 205.

10. Earl Pomeroy, *In Search of the Golden West: The Tourist in Western America* (New York: Alfred A. Knopf, 1957), 43.

11. Hans Huth, *Nature and the American: Three Centuries of Changing Attitudes* (Lincoln and London: University of Nebraska Press, 1972), 32.

12. Huth, *Nature and the American*, 84–86.

13. Pomeroy, *In Search of the Golden West*, 47–49.

14. Pomeroy, *In Search of the Golden West*, 5.

15. Alfred Runte, *National Parks: The American Experience* (Lincoln and London: University of Nebraska Press), 1979, chapter 1.

16. Roderick Nash, *Wilderness and the American Mind*, 3rd edition, (New Haven and London: Yale University Press, 1982), 80.

17. Foster, *The Civilized Wilderness*, 17.

18. Van Zandt, *The Catskill Mountain House*, 192.

19. Foster, *The Civilized Wilderness*, 18.

20. Hans Huth, *Yosemite: The Story of an Idea.* (Yosemite Natural History Association, 1964).

21. Hale, *Traits of American Life*. 1835, 187.

22. Van Zandt, *The Catskill Mountain House*, 212.

23. Act of June 30, 1864 (13 Stat. L., 325)—An Act Authorizing a grant to the State of California of the "Yo-Semite Valley" and of the land embracing the "Mariposa Big Tree Grove."

24. Huth, *Nature and the American*, 149.

25. Bowles, *Across the Continent,* 223.

26. Alfred Lambourne, *Pine Branches and Sea Weeds* (Salt Lake City: Donohue & Henneberry, 1889), 45.

27. J. D. Whitney, *The Yosemite Guide Book* (Cambridge: University Press, Welch, Bigelow, and Company, 1869), 80.

28. James M. Hutchings, *Scenes of Wonder and Curiosity in California: A Tourist Guide to the Yosemite Valley* (New York and San Francisco: A. Roman and Company, 1872), 113.

29. Bowles, *Across the Continent,* 226–227.

30. Hutchings, *Scenes of Wonder and Curiosity in California,* 124.

31. Hutchings, *Scenes of Wonder and Curiosity in California,* 123–124.

Chapter 3 *A Romantic Pleasure Resort*

1. King, *A Vacation Among The Sierras: Yosemite in 1860,* 65.

2. Hutchings, *Scenes of Wonder and Curiosity in California,* 158.

3. Fitz Hugh Ludlow, *The Heart of the Continent* (New York: Hurd and Houghton, 1870), 426.

4. Ludlow, *The Heart of the Continent,* 426.

5. Isaac H. Bromley, "The Big Trees and the Yosemite," *Scribner's Monthly* 3 (January 1872): 265–266.

6. Bromley, "The Big Trees and the Yosemite," 267.

7. Bromley, "The Big Trees and the Yosemite," 268.

8. *Report of the Commissioners to Manage the Yosemite Valley and the Mariposa Big Tree Grove.* (Sacramento: 1885–1886), 25. Hereafter listed as *Y.V.C.R.*

9. *Y.V.C.R.*, 1870–1871, 4–5.

10. *Y.V.C.R.*, 1874–1875, 4–5.

11. Shirley Sargent, *Galen Clark: Yosemite Guardian* (Yosemite: Flying Spur Press, 1981), 12.

12. *Y.V.C.R.*, 1880–1882, 19.

13. Samuel Kneeland, *The Wonders of the Yosemite Valley, and of California* (Boston: A. Moore, Lee and Shepard; New York: Lee Shepard and Dillingham, 1872), xi.

14. Pomeroy, *In Search of the Golden West,* introductory pictures, a Raymond and Whitcomb advertisement for Hotel Del Monte, Monterey, California.

15. Pomeroy, *In Search of the Golden West,* 9.

16. King, *A Vacation Among the Sierras: Yosemite in 1860,* 56, 62.

17. Whitney, *The Yosemite Guide Book,* 14.

18. Olive Logan, "Does It Pay To Visit Yo Semite?" *The Galaxy* 10 (October 1870): 506–507.

19. King, *A Vacation Among the Sierras: Yosemite in 1860,* 35.

20. Charles Warren Stoddard, "In Yosemite Shadows," *Overland Monthly* 3 (August 1869): 108.

21. Ludlow, *The Heart of the Continent,* 433.

22. Charles S. Greene, "Where the Gray Squirrel Hides," *Overland Monthly* 30 (July 1897): 62.

23. Pomeroy, *In Search of the Golden West,* 21.

24. Charles A. Bailey, "Unfrequented Paths of Yosemite," *Overland Monthly* 8 (July 1886): 88.

25. Pomeroy, *In Search of the Golden West,* 52.

26. Max O'Rell (Paul Blouet), *Jonathan and His Continent: Rambles Through American Society* (Bristol: Cassell and Company, 1889), 295.

27. Hutchings, *Scenes of Wonder and Curiosity in California,* 87, 112.

28. Carl P. Russell, *One Hundred Years in Yosemite* (Yosemite National Park: Yosemite Natural History Association, 1968), 103.

29. Logan, "Does It Pay To Visit Yo Semite?" 501–506.

30. Bromley, "The Big Trees and the Yosemite," 262.

31. C. F. Gordon-Cumming, *Granite Crags of California* (Edinburgh and London: William Blackwood & Sons, 1886), 91.

32. Logan, "Does It Pay To Visit Yo Semite?" 507–508.

33. Prentice Mulford, "The East at Yosemite," *Overland Monthly* 7 (August 1871): 194.

34. Sargent, *Galen Clark: Yosemite Guardian,* 17.

35. G. W. Steevens, *The Land of the Dollar,* 2nd edition, (Edinburgh: W. Blackwood and Sons,

1897), 253.

36. Pomeroy, *In Search of the Golden West*, introductory photos.

37. Mulford, "The East at Yosemite," 191.

38. Editorial in *Garden and Forest* (New York: The Garden and Forest Publishing Company, January 2, 1889), 1.

39. *Garden and Forest*, 1–2.

40. *Y.V.C.R.*, 1889–1890, 13, 15.

41. *Y.V.C.R.*, 1889–1890, 17.

42. *Y.V.C.R.*, 1889–1890, 23.

43. *Y.V.C.R.*, 1891–1892, 12.

44. *Y.V.C.R.*, 1891–1892, 15.

45. *Y.V.C.R.*, 1891–1892, 16.

46. *Y.V.C.R.*, 1893–1894, 7.

47. *Y.V.C.R.*, 1889–1890, 21.

48. *Y.V.C.R.*, 1891–1892, 9.

Chapter 4   *The Great Outdoors*

1. Nash, *Wilderness and the American Mind*, 145.

2. May King Van Rensselaer, *Newport: Our Social Capital* (New York: Arno Press, 1975), 81. Reprint of 1905 edition published by Lippincott, Philadelphia.

3. Pomeroy, *In Search of the Golden West*, 140–144.

4. Kevin Starr, *Americans and the California Dream, 1850–1915* (New York: Oxford University Press, 1973), 177.

5. Starr, *Americans and the California Dream*, 177.

6. Shirley Sargent, *John Muir in Yosemite* (Yosemite: Flying Spur Press, 1971), 5.

7. Nash, *Wilderness and the American Mind*, 160.

8. "About the Yosemite," *American Review of Reviews* 45 (1912): 766–767.

9. Starr, *Americans and the California Dream, 1850–1915*, 185.

10. D. J. Foley, *Yosemite Souvenir and Guide* (Yosemite: Tourists' Studio Office, 1912 ed.), 65–66.

11. Walter Laidlaw, "A Camping Tour to the Yosemite," *Outlook* 56 (June 5, 1897): 320.

12. "Impressions of a Careless Traveler," *The Outlook* 78 (Saturday, October 15, 1904): 413.

13. Laidlaw, "A Camping Tour to the Yosemite," 324.

14. Ramond H. Bailey, "Camping and Mountaineering in Yosemite National Park," in *Handbook of Yosemite National Park: A Compendium of Articles on the Yosemite Region by the Leading Scientific Authorities,* Ansel F. Hall, ed. (New York: Putnam, 1921), 271–272.

15. John Burroughs, "The Spell of the Yosemite," *Century* 81 n.s., (November 1910): 48.

16. *Y.V.C.R.*, 1893–1894, 10–11.

17. Lucius P. Deming, Judge of the Court of Common Pleas, New Haven, Connecticut, letter in *Century Magazine* 39 (January 1890) No. 3, 477.

18. A. J. Wells, *The Yosemite Valley of California* (Southern Pacific Railroad, 1905).

19. U. S. Department of the Interior. *Proceedings of the National Park Conference Held at the Yellowstone National Park, September 11 and 12, 1911* (Washington: U. S. Government Printing Office, 1912), 57. Hereafter cited as *Proceedings, N.P. Conf., 1911.*

20. "Report on Franchise Situation, Yosemite National Park" (Manuscript in Yosemite National Park Research Library, 1923).

21. Mary Curry Tresidder, "Early Days at Camp Curry," in *Yosemite: Saga of a Century, 1864-1964,* Jack Gyer, ed. (Oakhurst: The Sierra Star Press, 1964), 21.

22. L. M. Wetzel, "Impressions of a Visit to Yosemite," *Out West* 7 n.s., (1914): 138–139.

23. Wetzel, "Impressions of a Visit to Yosemite," 138–139.

24. *Y.V.C.R.*, 1901–1902, 6.

25. C. B. Bradley, "Knapsack Tours in the Sierra," *Sierra Club Bulletin* 1 (1893–1896): 314–315.

26. John Muir, from "Proceedings of the Meeting of the Sierra Club Held November 23, 1895," *Sierra Club Bulletin* 1 (January 1896): 280.

27. Ruth K. Wood, *The Tourist's California* (New York: Dodd, Mead, 1914), 201.

28. Foley, *Yosemite Souvenir and Guide*, 70.

29. Pomeroy, *In Search of the Golden West*, introductory photographs.

30. U. S. Department of the Interior. *Proceedings of the National Park Conference Held at the Yosemite National Park, October 14, 15, and 16, 1912* (Washington: U. S. Government Printing Office, 1913), 16. Hereafter cited as *Proceedings, N.P. Conf., 1912.*

31. William E. Colby, "Proposed Summer Outing of the Sierra Club," *Sierra Club Bulletin* 3 (1900–1901): 250–253.

32. "A Quarter-Century of Outings," *Sierra Club Bulletin* 12 (1927): 373.

33. Francis M. Fultz, "An Easterner's Impressions of a Sierra Club Outing," *Sierra Club Bulletin* 6 (1906–1908): 255.

34. E. T. Parsons, "The Sierra Club Outing to Tuolumne Meadows, (A Man's View of the Outing)," *Sierra Club Bulletin* 4 (1902–1903): 20–22.

35. Ella M. Sexton, "Camp Muir in the Tuolumne Meadows . . ," *Sierra Club Bulletin* 4 (January, 1902): 12.

36. Frank Soule, "Joseph LeConte in the Sierra," *Sierra Club Bulletin* 4 (1902): 2.

37. Marion Randall, "Some Aspects of a Sierra Club Outing," *Sierra Club Bulletin* 5 (1904–1905): 225.

38. U. S. Department of the Interior. *Proceedings of the National Park Conference Held at Berkeley, California, March 11, 12, and 13, 1915* (Washington: U. S. Government Printing Office, 1915), 32.

39. *Proceedings, N. P. Conf., 1911*, 109.

40. *Proceedings, N. P. Conf., 1911*, 119.

41. *Proceedings, N. P. Conf., 1911*, 149.

42. *Proceedings, N. P. Conf., 1911*, 149.

43. *Proceedings, N. P. Conf., 1912*, 141.

Chapter 5   *The Nation's Playgrounds*

1. Frank E. Brimmer, "Auto-Camping, the Fastest Growing Sport," *Outlook* 137 (July 16, 1924): 437.

2. U. S. Department of the Interior. *Report of the Director of the National Park Service to the Secretary of the Interior* (Washington: U. S. Government Printing Office, 1922), 14. Hereafter cited as *Report, Dir. NPS*, for respective years.

3. "The Cost of a Transcontinental Auto Journey," *Sunset* 53 (September 1924): 48–49.

4. *Report, Dir. NPS*, 1929, 149.

5. *Proceedings, N. P. Conf., 1911*, 17–18.

6. Robert Shankland, *Steve Mather of the National Parks* (New York: Alfred A. Knopf, 1951), 134.

7. *Report, Dir. NPS*, 1923, 4.

8. Shankland, *Steve Mather of the National Parks*, 134.

9. *The Ahwahnee* (Yosemite Park and Curry Company, n. d.)

10. *Report, Dir. NPS*, 1923, 54.

11. *Report, Dir. NPS*, 1929, 23.

12. Ansel F. Hall, ed. *Handbook of Yosemite National Park: A Compendium of Articles on the Yosemite Region by the Leading Scientific Authorities* (New York: Putnam, 1921), 82.

13. John Ise, *Our National Park Policy* (Baltimore: Johns Hopkins Press, 1961), 198.

14. John H. Williams, *Yosemite and its High Sierra* (San Francisco: John H. Williams, 1914), 66.

15. *Report, Dir. NPS*, 1922, 45.

16. *Report, Dir. NPS*, 1930, 170–171.

17. Jack Gyer, Ed., *Yosemite, Saga of a Century* (Oakhurst: The Sierra Star Press, 1964), 28.

18. Hall, *Handbook of Yosemite National Park*, 80.

19. Stephen T. Mather, "Educational Value of Parks," *Yosemite Nature Notes* 4 (May 1925): 33.

20. *Report, Dir. NPS*, 1926, 6.

21. *Report, Dir. NPS*, 1926, 34.

22. Harold C. Bryant and Wallace W. Atwood, *Research and Education in the National Parks* (Washington: U. S. Department of the Interior, 1932), 37.

23. *Report, Dir. NPS*, 1931, 19.

24. A. E. Borell, "History of Fishing in Yosemite," *Yosemite Nature Notes* 13 (August 1934): 107–109.

25. M. E. Beatty, "Bears of Yosemite," *Yosemite Nature Notes* 22 (January 1943): 14.

26. C. A. Harwell, "Our Changing Bears," *Yosemite Nature Notes* 16 (April 1937): 28.

27. Beatty, "Bears of Yosemite," 15.

28. *Report, Dir. NPS*, 1925, 11.

29. Lemuel A. Garrison, "Camper Activities in Yosemite Valley," *Yosemite Nature Notes* 18 (June 1939): 73.

30. Horace M. Albright and Frank J. Taylor, *"Oh, Ranger!" A Book About the National Parks* (Stanford University: Stanford University Press, 1929), 28.

31. Lemuel A. Garrison, *The Making of a Ranger: Forty Years with the National Parks* (Salt Lake City and Chicago: Howe Brothers, 1983), 132.

32. Garrison, "Camper Activities in Yosemite Valley," 74, 77.

33. Garrison, *The Making of a Ranger*, 308.

34. John H. Williams, *Yosemite and its High Sierra* (San Francisco: John H. Williams, 1921).

35. Shirley Sargent, *The Ahwahnee: Yosemite's Classic Hotel* (Yosemite: Yosemite Park and Curry Company, 1982), 20.

36. Sargent, *The Ahwahnee*, 20.

37. Robert E. Manning, "Men and Mountains Meet: Journal of the Appalachian Mountain Club, 1876–1984," *Journal of Forest History* 28 (January 1984): 27.

38. Ansel F. Hall, "High Sierra Camps," *Sierra Club Bulletin* 12 (1924): 39.

39. *Report, Dir. NPS*, 1929, 149–150.

40. Dorothy M. Emmet, "A British Student Looks at the Sierra Club," *Sierra Club Bulletin* 15 (1930): 24.

41. Charles A. Noble, "The Sierra Club Outing of 1919," *Sierra Club Bulletin* 11 (1920–23): 14.

42. Herbert O. Warren, "Snow Sports in California," *Country Life* 69 (1935): 67.

43. Hall, *Handbook of Yosemite National Park*, 83.

44. *Report, Dir. NPS*, 1930, 171.

45. Shirley Sargent, *Yosemite and Its Innkeepers: The Story of a Great Park and its Chief Concessionaires* (Yosemite: Flying Spur Press, 1975), 110.

46. Shirley Sargent, *Yosemite's High Sierra Camps* (Yosemite: Flying Spur Press, 1977), 14.

47. Warren James Belasco, *Americans on the Road: From Autocamp to Motel, 1910–1945* (Cambridge and London: The MIT Press), 1979, 74.

48. Bradford Torrey, *Field Days in California* (New York: Houghton Mifflin, 1913), 151–152.

49. Albright and Taylor, *"Oh, Ranger!"*, 5.

50. Donald C. Swain, *Wilderness Defender: Horace M. Albright and Conservation* (Chicago and London: University of Chicago Press, 1970), 170.

51. Horace M. Albright, letter to Robert Binneweis, August 12, 1981.

52. Stephen T. Mather, "Progress in the National Parks," *Sierra Club Bulletin* 11 (1920–23): 7.

53. Hall, *Handbook of Yosemite National Park*, 84–85.

54. Albright and Taylor, *"Oh, Ranger!"*, 135.

55. Allan Kress Fitzsimmons, "The Effect of the Automobile on the Cultural Elements of the Landscape of Yosemite Valley" (MA Thesis, San Fernando Valley State College, Department of Geography, 1969), 48.

56. Garrison, *The Making of a Ranger*, 101.

57. Hall, *Handbook of Yosemite National Park*, 46.

58. John A. Jakle, *The Tourist: Travel in Twentieth-Century North America* (Lincoln and London: University of Nebraska Press, 1985), 67.

59. F. Fraser Darling and Noel D. Eichhorn, *Man and Nature in the National Parks* (Washington: The Conservation Foundation, 1967), 22.

60. Charles J. Finger, *Foot-Loose in the West* (New York: Morrow, 1932), 221.

Chapter 6   *The Wilderness Era*

1. Charles Stevenson, "The Shocking Truth About Our National Parks," *Reader's Digest* 66 (January 1955): 45.
2. Bernard DeVoto, "Let's Close the National Parks," *Harper's Magazine* 207 (October 1953): 51.
3. Roland Steinmetz, "Some Aspects of Mission 66," Part I, *Yosemite Nature Notes* 36 (September 1957): 87–88, 100.
4. Garrison, *The Making of a Ranger*, 257.
5. Ronald F. Lee, *Public Use of the National Park System, 1872–2000* (Washington: U. S. Department of the Interior, National Park Service, 1968), 6.
6. 78 Stat. 890–896 (1964), 16 U.S.C. 1131–1136 (1965).
7. Starr Jenkins, "Down With Yosemite City!" *San Francisco Magazine* 7 (August 1965) No. 8.
8. Devereux Butcher, *Exploring Our National Parks and Monuments* (New York: Oxford University Press, 1947), 86.
9. Alexander B.Adams, ed., *First World Conference on National Parks: Proceedings* (U. S. Department of the Interior, National Park Service, 1964), 172–173.
10. Bruce L. Fincham, "Visitor Survey in Yosemite Valley, Yosemite National Park, California, With Emphasis on Trail Use" (MA Thesis, The Pennsylvania State University, Department of Forestry and Wildlife, 1968), 37.
11. Darling and Eichhorn, *Man and Nature in the National Parks*, 40–42, 60.
12. Adams, *First World Conference on National Parks*, 47–48.
13. Chris Jones, *Climbing in North America* (Berkeley and Los Angeles: University of California Press, 1976), 365.
14. *Report, Dir. NPS*, 1972, 6.
15. David Schonauer, "The Base Case," *Outside* (April 1983): 56, 59.
16. Conrad L. Wirth, *Parks, Politics, and the People* (Norman: University of Oklahoma Press, 1980), 61.
17. Steinmetz, "Some Aspects of Mission 66," 87–88, 100.
18. Garrison, *The Making of a Ranger*, 259.
19. Nathaniel T. Kenney, "The Other Yosemite," *National Geographic* 145 (June 1974): 774.
20. George B. Hartzog, Jr., "Clearing the Roads—and the Air—in Yosemite Valley," *National Parks and Conservation Magazine* (August 1972): 14, 17.
21. Jan W. van Wagtendonk, "Visitor Use Patterns in Yosemite National Park," *Journal of Travel Research*, (Fall 1980), 15.

Chapter 7   *Epilogue*

1. Lemuel A. Garrison, "Practical Experience in Standards, Policies, and Planning," in *First World Conference on National Parks: Proceedings*, Alexander B. Adams, ed. (U. S. Department of the Interior, National Park Service, 1964,) 195–196.
2. Lee, *Public Use of the National Park System, 1872–2000*, 17.
3. *National Parks for the Future* (Washington: The Conservation Foundation, 1972), 153–154.
4. David Sumner, "What's Next for Yosemite?" *National Wildlife* 15 (October–November 1977): 37.
5. *National Parks for the Future*, 131.
6. Ise, *Our National Park Policy*, 647–648.
7. Hartzog, "Clearing the Roads—and the Air—in Yosemite Valley," 17.

Index